Grass Will Not Grow On My Grave

The Story of the Appin Murder

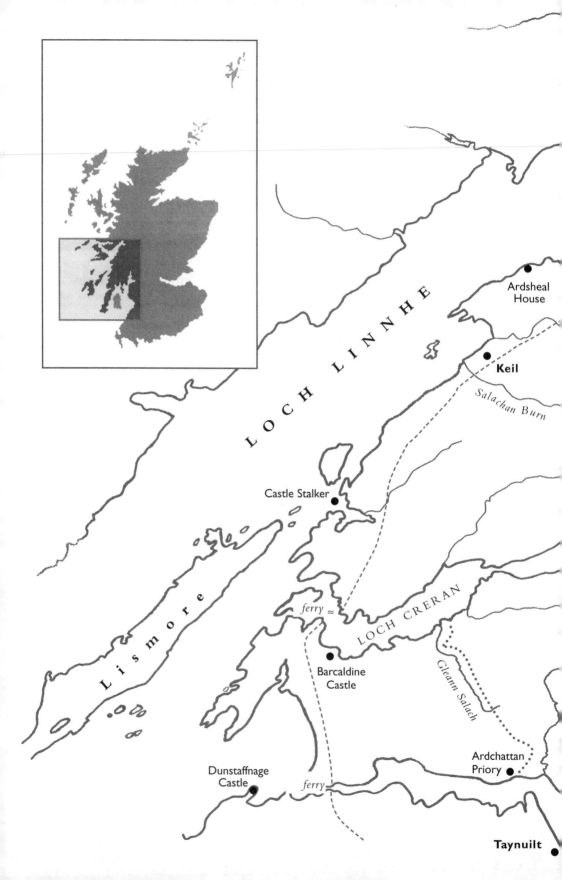

Ardsheal
House

Keil

Salachan Burn

LOCH LINNHE

Castle Stalker

L i s m o r e

ferry ≈

LOCH CRERAN

Barcaldine
Castle

Gleann Salach

Ardchattan
Priory

Dunstaffnage
Castle

ferry

Taynuilt

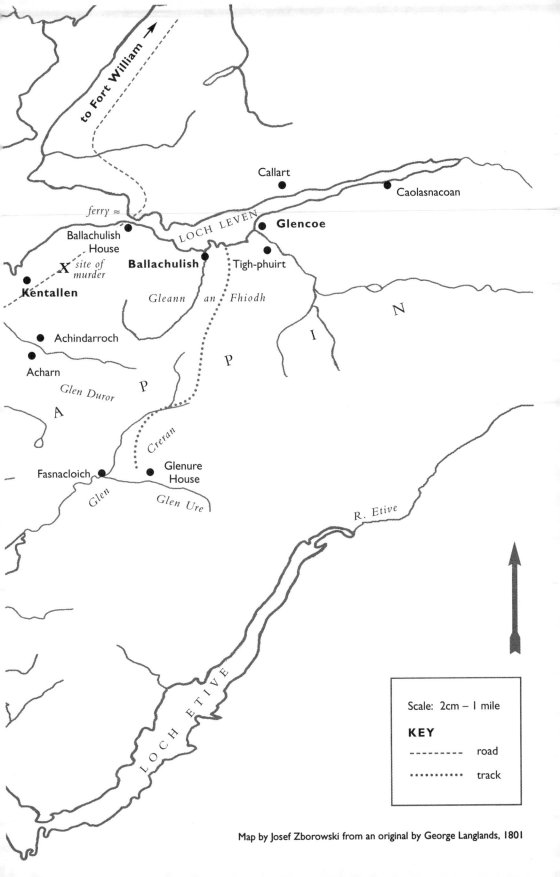

to Fort William →

Callart

Caolasnacoan

ferry ≈

LOCH LEVEN

Glencoe

Ballachulish
House

X site of
murder

Ballachulish

Tigh-phuirt

Kentallen

Gleann an Fhiodh

N

Achindarroch

I

P

P

Acharn

Glen Duror

A

Creran

Fasnacloich

Glenure
House

Glen

Glen Ure

R. Etive

LOCH ETIVE

Scale: 2cm – 1 mile

KEY

- - - - - - - - - road

• • • • • • • • • track

Map by Josef Zborowski from an original by George Langlands, 1801

First published in 2002 and reprinted in 2003 by

SCOTTISH CULTURAL PRESS

Unit 6, Newbattle Abbey Business Park
Newbattle Road, DALKEITH EH22 3LJ Scotland
Tel: +44 (0)131 660 6366 • Fax: +44 (0)131 660 4666
Email: info@scottishbooks.com

website: www.scottishbooks.com

BRITISH LIBRARY CATALOGUING IN PUBLICATION DATA
A catalogue record for this book is available from the British Library

ISBN: 1 84017 047 6

Printed and bound by Bell & Bain Ltd, Glasgow

Grass will not Grow on my Grave

The Story of the Appin Murder

'Ma tha mi neochiontach cha'n fhàs feur air m'uaigh'
'If I am innocent, grass will not grow on my grave'

Prophesy of Seumas a' Ghlinne, James of the Glen,
before he was hanged on 8 November, 1752

SCOTTISH CULTURAL PRESS

Note on the Author

Mary McGrigor grew up in a fifteenth-century Scottish castle where she was captivated by a sense of the past. Authors like Scott and Buchan, and particularly R. L. Stevenson, increased her love of history and inspired an ambition to write. She married a soldier and 'followed the drum' until they bought a sheep farm in Argyll.

Her first book, *The History of South Lochaweside*, written for a SWRI (Scottish Women's Institute) competition, was followed by *Dalmally and the Glens*. She then became a regular contributor to *Scottish Field* magazine, before writing *Argyll, Land of Blood and Beauty*. She has edited *The Family of Edmonstone of Duntreath* and *The Scalpel and the Sword*, the autobiography of her husband's famous ancestor, Sir James McGrigor, 'father' of the Royal Army Medical Corps.

Grass will not Grow on my Grave investigates the notorious Appin Murder and the trial of James Stewart of the Glen. She is currently collaborating with the photographer Malcolm MacGregor on *Rob Roy's Country*, also to be published by Scottish Cultural Press.

Acknowledgements

My deepest thanks to Lady Stewart of Appin for so graciously writing the Foreword to this book. Also to the very Reverend Norman MacCallum, Provost of St John's Cathedral, Oban, and his wife, Barbara, for their fund of local knowledge; to Alastair Campbell of Airds, Unicorn Pursuivant, for his expert advice; to Archie MacKenzie, editor of *Scottish Field*, for the Gaelic translations; to photographers Malcolm MacGregor, Roy Summers and Gordon Ross Thomson; to Mr and Mrs Howard Bennett; to the Hon. Lord Weir; to Jamie and Sarah Troughton of Ardchattan; to Janet Summerlin; to Brian Pugh and Avril Gray of Scottish Cultural Press; to Andrew Hillhouse for the cover painting; to Eleanor Harris, Local Studies Librarian, and her colleague Neil MacIntyre; and also to the many other people who have helped me with advice and encouragement for this book.

CONTENTS

FOREWORD *by Lady Stewart of Appin*   11
INTRODUCTION   13

CHAPTER 1   15
Road to Lettermore
The Seeds of Discord Sown & the
Struggle for Supremacy in Lorn

CHAPTER 2   41
Jacobite Rising of 1745
The Men of Argyll Divided by
Loyalty to King and Prince

CHAPTER 3   51
The Men Who Took to the Hills

CHAPTER 4   55
The Farmer called Seumas a' Ghlinne

CHAPTER 5   63
Forfeiture of the Jacobite Estates

CHAPTER 6   74
James of the Glen's Attempt to Save
the Tenants of Ardsheal

CHAPTER 7   80
Pursuit Unseen

CHAPTER 8   85
Death on the Road through Lettermore

CHAPTER 9   96
No Name upon the Stone

CHAPTER 10   102
The Nights of Fear

CHAPTER 11   111
Imprisonment of James of the Glen

CHAPTER 12   117
The Trial of James Stewart

CHAPTER 13   129
The Execution

CHAPTER 14   132
Who Fired the Fatal Shot?

EPILOGUE   144

APPENDIX   145
The Speech of James Stewart
from the Scaffold

SELECT BIBLIOGRAPHY   153

INDEX   155

FOREWORD

It was with great pleasure that I accepted Mary McGrigor's request to write a Foreword to her excellent and much researched book on the Appin Murder, which has mystified this country for nigh on 250 years.

The truth of the incident has been handed down by each succeeding Chief of the Stewarts of Appin to this day.

Sibyl Anne Stewart
Lady Stewart of Appin
Salachail
Appin

Introduction

The ghastly figure on the gibbet stood black against the sky. In the high winds, the bones, wired together, rattled as though in a macabre dance of death. Local people, forced by necessity to go to and fro on the Ballachulish Ferry, shuddered and looked away. Many among them thought, 'there but for the grace of God go I,' but most felt a deep sorrow for the dead man, James of the Glen, hanged for a crime that they knew he did not commit. *Seumas a' Ghlinne*, as they knew him, had been a good man; he had not deserved such an end.

But then, neither had Colin Campbell of Glenure, of whose murder James Stewart had been found guilty 'in art and part'. During their lifetime the two had been more than neighbours; they had been friends. Now one hung as a warning to all enemies of the government of what their fate might be. Why did each man suffer such a terrible death? The answer lies partly in the long-running feud between the Campbells and the Stewarts, the roots of which lie buried deep in the past.

The area known as Appin is one of the loveliest parts of

Scotland. Lying at the north-west corner of the district of Lorn, it is sheltered on the east by the massive range of hills which tower above Glencoe. Wooded glens run down to the shores of Loch Linnhe where grass grows largely free of frost during the winter months.

The long, winding strath of Glen Creran divides Appin from the district of Ardchattan. During the eighteenth century this glen formed the boundary of the lands of the Stewarts and the Campbells, who by then held monopoly over most of Argyll. The loyalty of one clan to the Prince whose name they bore, and of the other to the Hanoverian king, resulted in the conflict that made enemies of former friends.

Mary McGrigor
Upper Sonachan
Argyll

CHAPTER 1

Road to Lettermore
The Seeds of Discord Sown & The
Struggle for Supremacy in Lorn

C olin, Lord Campbell – created Earl of Argyll in 1457 – was a man who thirsted for land. Already in possession of most of the country around and south of Loch Awe, he aspired for total control of the territory which bore his name.

The Lordship of Lorn, the northern part of Argyll, once held by the MacDougall Lords of Lorn, had passed through marriage to the Stewarts of Innermeath. John Stewart, Lord of Lorn, had three daughters and, since he had no legitimate son, they would inherit his estate. Argyll married Isabel, the second daughter; Colin Campbell of Glenorchy took Margaret, the eldest; and Arthur Campbell of Otter courted and wed the youngest, Marion. Adding these lands to his existing territory, Argyll now looked upon himself as lord of all Lorn.

Then, to his utter fury, his plan seemed about to fall apart. John Stewart's wife died and he announced that he would marry the daughter of MacLaren of Ardveich; that is, the mother of his illegitimate son, Dugald, who would thus become his heir.

The Campbells, determined to prevent this at any cost, hired a reprobate called Alan MacCoul to assassinate Stewart before the wedding could take place. MacCoul and his ruffians came in by sea under cover of darkness and hid close by, among the trees near Dunstaffnage Castle. Next day, as the wedding party walked from the castle to the family chapel, MacCoul and his men sprang out with daggers raised. They stabbed Stewart repeatedly, leaving him, or so they thought, for dead.

Some of his companions, however, realising he was just alive, carried him into the chapel where, with his last breath, he whispered the marriage vows.

Intermittent fighting followed between Dugald Stewart and Clan Campbell. The Campbells, swearing that the marriage had never taken place and declaring Dugald illegitimate, named Walter Stewart, his uncle, as the heir to the Lordship of Lorn. This had been the Campbell plan all along: the cunning Earl of Argyll had previously made an agreement with Walter Stewart whereby he promptly handed over Lorn to the Campbells in return for land in Perthshire and for their future support.

Dugald appealed to the Privy Council and eventually an agreement was reached. He would have Appin, the north-west part of Lorn, to be held directly from the Crown. Dugald had to be satisfied with this, but the seeds of antagonism had been sown.

In 1468 the intermittent fighting between the Campbells and the Stewarts of Appin was brought to a head when the Earl of Argyll and Walter Stewart decided to force the issue with an overwhelming strength of arms. Alan MacCoul (assassin of

John Stewart, Lord of Lorn) was put in charge of a large army of mercenaries paid to invade Appin.

Dugald Stewart, warned of what was happening, summoned the MacLarens to his aid. Cunningly, he deployed his force along the ridge, below which now stands the Episcopalian Church of Portnacroish. MacCoul and his men were hemmed in by the sea as the Stewarts and MacLarens swept down in an overwhelming charge. The battle became a bloodbath and, in the midst of it, Dugald cornered MacCoul and slew him, and so avenged his father's death.

The Battle of Stalk, as this was called, established 22-year-old Dugald Stewart's hold over Appin, although thanks to his uncle, Walter Stewart, he never regained the rest of Lorn.

On 14 April, 1470, Walter Stewart, as previously arranged, resigned the title and lands of Lorn, with Appin excluded, to the young King James III. Three days later, the King granted the Lordship of Lorn to Argyll. Argyll then gave a third of Lorn to his uncle, Sir Colin Campbell, 1st of Glenorchy. Significantly, the six merklands of Barcaldine were included. This land, in the district of Benderloch, lies south of Loch Creran and this was the site, it is believed, that Sir Colin chose to build his stronghold, probably near or on the site of the present castle of Barcaldine. From here he commanded the road from Connel Ferry to Appin. Argyll was making certain that his kinsman controlled the area to the north of Loch Etive.

Castle Stalker

Hunting Lodge of Two Stewart Kings

Dugald, first of the Stewart chiefs of Appin, lived until 1497. He died fighting. His mother's people, the MacLarens, had lifted cattle from the MacDonalds of Keppoch. They had crossed the Moor of Rannoch with the MacDonalds in pursuit. Dugald discovered what was happening and realised that the MacLarens were outnumbered. He sent his swiftest runner to announce he was coming to their aid. Raising his fighting men, he marched through Glencoe (where the local MacDonalds offered no resistance) and descended over the Black Mount to the head of Glenorchy, where he was joined by the MacLarens. Together, they made a dawn raid on the MacDonalds and in the ensuing skirmish Dugald was killed.

He was succeeded by his eldest son, Duncan, who formed a great friendship with the young King James IV. James was the first of the Stewarts to take a personal interest in the West Highlands. He learnt to speak some Gaelic before summoning the rebellious MacDonalds and other chiefs to a court at Dunstaffnage Castle in 1493.

Tall and athletic, the young king loved hunting and falconry, and in Duncan Stewart he found a kindred spirit with an energy to match his own. He also found a staunchly loyal subject; a valuable ally in the monarch's struggle to establish his authority in a sea girt part of his realm. It is thought that it was on the king's insistence, and perhaps with his financial help, that Duncan began renovating an ancient island fort.

There has probably been some sort of defence on *Creag an Sgairbh* (the Cormorant's Rock) since before recorded time.

Today, Castle Stalker, or *Castle Stalcaire*, as it is known in Gaelic, is one of the best-known landmarks in Argyll.

A Royal Charter, dated 14 January 1500, confirmed Duncan's superiority of all Appin, including Ballachulish and Lismore. Shortly afterwards, the king ordered Sir Duncan Campbell, 2nd of Glenorchy, to relinquish his holding of the southern part of Appin and a third of the island of Lismore. Later, on 24 September 1501, Archibald, 2nd Earl of Argyll, now the King's Lieutenant of Argyll, and Duncan Campbell of Glenorchy formally recognised Duncan Stewart, 2nd of Appin, as lord of the whole of Appin and Lismore, which he held directly from the Crown.

The King then made Duncan Stewart his Chamberlain of the Isles and, in addition, on 9 July 1512, he granted him the life rent of Inverlochy and part of Mamore. This was too much for some of the chiefs of other larger clans who thought the King's favouritism unjust. Lachlan MacLean of Duart, in particular, who had been promised the lands in Lochaber, felt himself grossly misused. He invited Duncan Stewart to his home in Duart, on Mull. According to legend, Duncan was unwise enough to travel there with only one attendant, named Sorley MacColl. During the journey, Sorley was set upon by some Macleans and Duncan, in trying to save him, was killed and left lying on the shore. His body, rescued by the MacLeay of Bachuill (ancestor of the Livingstones of Lismore) lies buried in the white-washed church of St Moluag on Lismore.

He was succeeded by his brother, Alan, who is thought to have completed the building of Castle Stalker. Thanks to careful restoration by Lt. Colonel Stewart Allward and his family, the castle we see today is much as it would have been in Alan's time.

The Battle of Flodden

Division of Land by Alan Stewart, 3rd of Appin

On the summons to arms of James IV, Alan, with his five sons, led the Stewarts of Appin to fight on the right wing of the royal army at the Battle of Flodden. Against the odds, they all survived and on his return Alan divided his land amongst his sons. Duncan, the eldest, became the heir to Appin; John was given Strathgarry; Achnacone went to Dugald; Fasnacloich to James and Invernahyle to Alexander. And so, in 1513, the first branches of the Clan Stewart of Appin were defined.

In 1538, King James V granted a new charter of the lands of Duror to 'his much beloved kinsman', Alan Stewart of Appin, to be held in hereditary directly from the Crown.

The Battle of Pinkie

*Grant of Ballachulish by Allan, 3rd of Appin,
to his Grandson*

In 1547, the Stewarts of Appin fought for James V at the Battle of Pinkie. Their force was commanded by Alan's grandson *Domhnull-nan-Ord* (Donald of the Hammers) – so named because he had been raised by a blacksmith – now 2nd of Invernahyle. The battle proved a crushing defeat: due to the poor leadership of the Earl of Arran, thousands of Scottish lives were lost. Donald's third son, however, fought valiantly and survived. When he returned home, his great-grandfather Alan, recognising his worth, granted him the land round Ballachulish, placing him in a position to guard the ferry across the mouth of Loch Leven – a main route to and from the north. The cadet branch of Clan Appin – the Stewarts of Ballachulish – was thus established in 1547.

Already settled in Ballachulish were several MacColl families (their common ancestor is said to have been 'Black Solomon', grandson of John, 1st Lord of the Isles), whose traditional claim on the holding round Ballachulish and Duror dated from *c*.1360. Likewise, the MacGillemichaels (or 'Carmichaels') were granted land at much the same time.

The association of these families with the Stewarts of Appin, continuing through succeeding generations, was eventually, in the case of the MacColls, to lead to betrayal and death.

Duart Castle, on the island of Mull
(photograph by Gordon Ross Thomson)

STEWARTS OF APPIN
~ FAMILY TREE ~

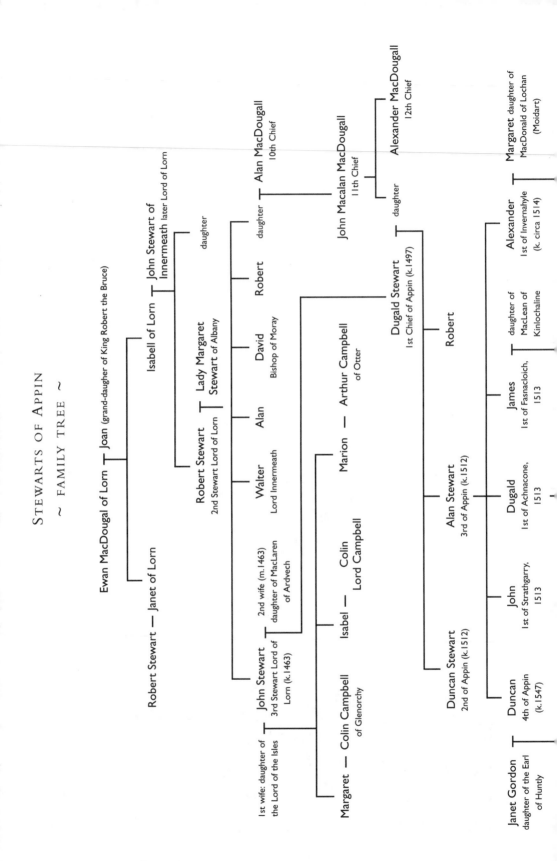

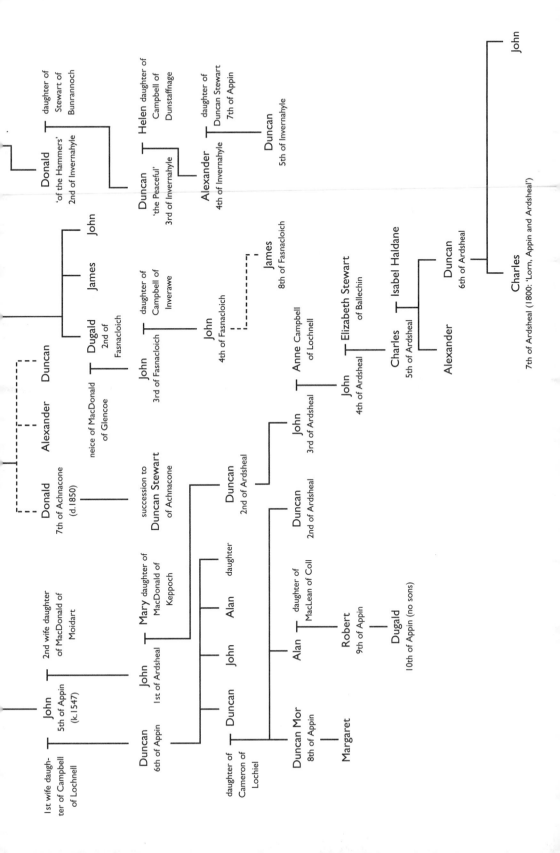

The Great Contract

The Murder of the Bonny Earl of Moray and of
Sir John Campbell of Calder and the Attempted
Assassination of Archibald, 7th Earl of Argyll

Alan Stewart, who lived to a great age, was succeeded as chief of Appin by his grandson, John Gordonich Ban (his mother was a Gordon) in 1562. John married Kathleen, daughter of Campbell of Lochnell, and through this union became involved in the infamous scheme to murder both Sir John Campbell of Calder and the young 7th Earl of Argyll.

Colin, 6th Earl of Argyll, had died in his early forties in September 1584, but not before he had made a will instructing his widow, Agnes, to take charge of their two sons and his vast estates. He stated that she was to be aided in this formidable task by a cohort of Campbell chiefs, together with Neil Campbell of Ederline, Bishop of Argyll. The chiefs he named were Duncan Campbell of Glenorchy, Dougal Campbell of Auchinbreck, John Campbell of Calder, Sir James Campbell of Ardkinlass[1] (controller to the King), and Archibald Campbell of Lochnell. In a final clause, however, he decreed that documents could only be legalised by Campbell of Calder, Campbell of Ardkinlass and the bishop.

This caused great offence to Archibald Campbell of Lochnell, who, as next in line to the earldom of Argyll (in the event of the demise of the late Earl's two young sons), believed himself entitled to the seat of power. He soon saw a chance to avenge himself by becoming embroiled in the continuing controversy between George Gordon, Earl of Huntly, and James Stewart, Earl of Moray, over possession of the earldom of

[1] 'Calder' is the old spelling of 'Cawdor'. Ardkinlass, sometimes spelt 'Ardkinglass', is an estate on the south-east shore of Loch Fyne.

Moray. This valuable land, adjoining the Moray Firth, had been held by the Gordons since 1562 when Mary Queen of Scots gave it to her half-brother, James Stewart. Stewart, who became Regent following the Queen's abdication, was murdered in 1569. His eldest daughter, Elizabeth, succeeded him as Countess of Moray in her own right and transferred her title to her husband, James Stewart, Lord Doune, who thus became Earl of Moray.

In the instance of the dispute over the earldom of Huntly, Sir John Campbell of Calder obeyed the wishes of the Countess of Argyll, who naturally supported the claims of her daughter and son-in-law. Calder may not have realised that in doing so he was laying himself open to the machinations of Campbell of Lochnell and the other unscrupulous and ambitious men with whom he was involved.

Foremost amongst these was Sir Duncan Campbell, 7th knight (later 1st baronet) of Glenorchy, who was known for his habit of wearing a skull cap as 'Black Duncan of the Cowl'.[2] Glenorchy, already renowned as one of the cleverest and most devious men in Scotland, was at that time systematically evicting the people of Clan Gregor from Glenstrae at the head of Loch Awe. Local landlords who had helped these unfortunate people, largely because they needed fighting men, included Campbell of Calder. So, for this reason, Glenorchy had already found a cause for dispute. Now he seized upon the chance to support Lochnell, while at the same time intriguing with Sir James Campbell of Ardkinlass, who also resented Calder's predominance over the Countess of Argyll.

The quarrel between Calder and Ardkinlass reached a point where each tried to kill the other. Neither succeeded. Ardkinlass died of natural causes in 1591 but his son, notorious

[2] Or 'Black Duncan of the Hood'.

for being weak-minded and easily led, carried on the family feud.

Assured of Huntly's backing, Lochnell, began to rally local lairds who resented Calder's self-appointed mastery over the Argyll estates. Foremost among them was John Stewart, 5th of Appin, who, his mother being a Gordon and his wife a Campbell of Lochnell, had two good reasons to side with Lochnell. Others who joined the conspiracy included Lachlan MacLean of Duart – whose ancestor had been slain by Calder's grandfather – and Duncan MacDougall of Dunollie. Encouraged by this support, the conspirators inveigled two men in high office into their sinister web. One was none other than the Lord Chancellor, John Maitland, Lord Thirlestane. The other was William Douglas, Earl of Morton – the same man who had held Queen Mary prisoner in his island castle in Loch Leven in 1567. These men pledged themselves to the destruction, not only of Calder and Moray, but of the young Earl of Argyll and his brother Colin as well.

Considered in retrospect, the enormity of their proposed crimes seems barely comprehensible until it becomes obvious that Lochnell and Glenorchy were acting with the main objective of gaining control of Argyll. The proposed killing of Moray and Calder, while providing a reason for rallying support, was to them of secondary importance. Their main goal was to dispose of the two young Campbells of Argyll. They had already divided the spoils, striking a bargain by which Lochnell, having inherited the earldom, would then grant Glenorchy his much coveted Lordship of Loch Awe.

The plan agreed, the Gordons were the first to act. George Gordon, Earl of Huntly, had received a commission from King James VI to arrest supporters of Francis Stewart, Earl of

Bothwell, who had raided Holyrood House. Armed with the royal warrant, he seized the long-awaited chance to avenge the deaths of his father and two brothers. Their murders had been contrived by Moray's father-in-law, Lord James Stewart, who, with Queen Mary's approval, had also taken their land.

It was February. Darkness fell early. On the night of the 7th, Huntly rode down into Fife with a band of armed men. Moray's castle of Donibristle stood above the sea. Huntly's men set fire to it by shooting arrows tipped with flaming tar into the roof and piling burning wood against the timber door. Moray, sleeping in an upstairs chamber, was woken by the noise and the smoke. Leaping from his bed, he somehow managed to get out of the castle and scramble down to the shore. Stumbling on stones, slipping on seaweed, he thought he had escaped in the darkness, but a spark had ignited the silken tassel on his night-cap. Huntly's men, yelling like hounds at sight of their quarry, pursued the bobbing light. Overtaking him, they showed no mercy; they literally hacked him to death.

Then it was Calder's turn to die.

Campbell of Ardkinlass, with the help of John Oig Campbell of Cabrachan, a brother of Lochnell, found a man called MacKellar who agreed to shoot Calder for a reward. Ardkinlass provided a hagbut – a long-barrelled gun or 'musket' (also called an 'arquebus') – which was largely used for shooting birds and deer. MacKellar waited until word came that Calder was at his house of Knepoch[3] on the south shore of Loch Feochan, some three miles from where the town of Oban stands today.

MacKellar waited for darkness with Knepoch House in view. Silently, he crept upon it, guided by the candlelight from an unshuttered window. Raising himself to the level of the sill,

[3] Knepoch is now called 'Knipoch' and lies on south shore of Loch Feochan. The old house is incorporated within the building of the present-day hotel.

he spied his target within. He fired three shots, reloading quickly, and saw Calder fall and die.

Despite the resulting commotion, MacKellar escaped into the night. A boat may have been waiting for him as MacDougall of Dunollie (whose castle, now ruined, stands above Oban Bay) protected him for some time. Later, however, both MacKellar and John Oig Campbell of Cabrachan were arrested and imprisoned by the Campbells. John Oig, tortured by a hideous contraption called the 'boot', which drove nails into the victim's legs, confessed to his own involvement and to that of Lochnell and Dunollie. Both he and MacKellar were executed, but thanks to some powerful influence (doubtless that of Thirlestane and Morton), Lochnell and Dunollie, although for some time imprisoned, escaped the capital punishment which Lochnell, at any rate, deserved.

Archibald Campbell, the young Earl of Argyll, aware of the feud between Calder and Ardkinlass, vowed to wreck vengeance on the latter. In his desperation, Ardkinlass resorted to consulting witches and sought the help of Margaret Campbell, widow of the conspirator John Oig. Glenorchy then tried to involve him in a scheme to kill Argyll and his brother, offering land, which included part of Rosneath, as reward. However, Ardkinlass, by now utterly terrified, refused to have any part in this scheme.

In May 1594, the witches having proved useless and tortured by his conscience, Ardkinlass confessed to all that he knew, not only of the plots against Calder but of the 'great contract' to kill both Moray and Argyll. His story, corroborated by Margaret Campbell (procurer of the witches) provides the greatest evidence of the plot. A special commission was issued for the trial of Ardkinlass but, having turned King's evidence, he was spared.

Argyll remained in ignorance of the schemes of Lochnell and Glenorchy. In the spring of 1594 (almost at the same time as Ardkinlass was telling what he knew) Argyll was in Stirling. His servants had been bribed to poison him and he was seriously ill.

The death of Moray, at the hands of Huntly, had resulted in much disturbance in the Highlands amongst the rival supporters of both earls. Rumour ran wild that Huntly, together with the Catholic earls of Angus and Errol, was intriguing with Philip of Spain to effect a Catholic reformation in Scotland. In June 1594 they forcibly freed some Catholics who had been imprisoned by the magistrates of Aberdeen. King James VI commissioned three Protestant lords – Argyll, Atholl and Forbes – to subdue the rebel force. Argyll, now a forceful figure, although only seventeen, marched north with a force of over six thousand men. At Glenlivet he took up a strong position to confront Huntly's army, which was smaller than his own.

Lochnell, his treachery apparently undetected, was one of Argyll's commanders. Secretly, he sent a message to Huntly telling him to make his gunners aim at the white and yellow standard of Argyll. Perhaps they were inaccurate or the cannon ball ricocheted off the ground. Whatever actually happened, the shots missed their target. Argyll was unhurt while Lochnell himself was killed.

John Stewart of Appin escaped retribution for his involvement with his kinsman, Lochnell. Nonetheless, 'the assassination of Calder caused a feud between the Stewarts of Appin and the Campbells of Calder's house, the effects of which were long felt.'[4]

[4] From Gregory Donald's *History of the Western Highlands and Isles of Scotland*, p. 255.

John Stewart, 5th of Appin, married twice. By his second wife, a daughter of MacDonald of Moidart, he had a son, John, who became the first Stewart of Ardsheal.

Sir Duncan Campbell of the Castles

In Appin, the influence of Sir Duncan Campbell, 7th of Glenorchy, was more immediately felt. 'Black Duncan of the Cowl' was one of the most remarkable men of his day. A renowned tyrant, he was also a leading agriculturist and silviculturist, as well as a collector of books and works of art. He is famous as 'Duncan of the Castles' on account of the seven fortalices which he either built or restored. The castles, placed at strategic points, were garrisoned and held armouries from which, in times of emergency, the local men were equipped with targes (small, round shields also known as 'bucklers'), axes and pikes.

One of the castles which he built was Barcaldine Castle, in Benderloch, which was finished in 1609. Standing on a low ridge near to the south shore of Loch Creran, it commanded the approach to the South Shian Ferry on the old road from Connel Ferry to Appin. According to *The Black Book of Taymouth* (the records of the Campbells of Glenorchy), Sir Duncan 'biggit ane greit hows in Benderloch in Lorne of four hows heicht, the largest hows theiroff woltit, for the workmanship quhairoff he gaif fyve thowsand markis, anno 1601. Item he biggit the howss of Barcaltane in Lorne and endit it anno 1609.'

In 1621, Barcaldine was given to Patrick Campbell, Sir Duncan's natural son. A later grant of 1642 included the obligation to entertain Sir Robert Campbell of Glenorchy (Duncan's grandson), who in turn agreed to 'uphold and hold watertight the said manor place of Barchaltan upone his owne expensse'.[5]

Sir Donald Campbell of Ardnamurchan

A Castle for a Boat

Duncan, 7th of Appin, was known as Duncan *Baothaire* (weak-minded). In financial difficulties, he sold all the land south and west of the village of Appin to Sir Donald Campbell of Ardnamurchan in 1627. This man, originally known as Donald Campbell of Barbreck Loch Awe, was the natural son of Sir John Campbell of Calder, murdered in his house of Knepoch through the conniving of Campbell of Lochnell, John Stewart's brother-in-law.

Donald Campbell had greatly advanced his fortunes by making astute land deals. His agreement with Duncan Baothaire must have seemed just revenge for any association that the young man's father may have had with the assassination of his own. Knowing that Duncan had a weakness for drink he saw how to further his aims.

Duncan had a great fancy for a birlinn (an eight-oared galley) which Sir Donald possessed. Donald, knowing this, entertained him lavishly to the point where Duncan Stewart was completely fuddled by wine. In this state, he agreed to exchange his castle for the boat. Next morning, when he was sober, he tried desperately to rescind the agreement but Sir Donald claimed the castle as his own.

The New Statistical Account of 1845 states that the

[5] Scottish Record Office, Breadalbane Collection, GD 112/10/1, Tacks.

building was 'new roofed and floored' by Sir Donald Campbell of Ardnamurchan in 1631. The alterations he made were specifically for defence. The top floor, which contained a garret chamber, was surrounded by a parapet walk; the outer wall was pierced with gun-loops and pistol-holes. A narrow stone stair from the north-west walk led to a cap house above the stair head. Also, as an added precaution, the drawbridge was designed to hinge downwards within the supporting timber frame.[6] Shortly afterwards, however, the wooden staircase to the front entrance was replaced by the stone one we see today and the drawbridge subsequently removed.

The Civil Wars

1643–1689

The Civil war between Charles I and his Parliament broke out in England in 1642. In 1644, the Marquis of Montrose, created Lieutenant-General of the Royalist forces in Scotland, was joined by a force from Ireland commanded by the distinguished soldier Alasdair MacColla MacDonald.

Alasdair landed in Ardnamurchan where the local people were too terrified of their landlord, Sir Donald Campbell, to rise in arms for the King. Alasdair, however, joined Montrose at Blair Atholl and together they won the succession of victories for which they will always be famed. In December 1644 they invaded Argyll, and the Marquis of Argyll only just escaped from Inveraray in a fishing boat, leaving the little town in flames.

[6] From the Register of the Privy Council of Scotland, 1684.

Situated on *Creag an Sgairbh* (the Cormorant's Rock), Castle Stalker, or
Castle Stalcaire as it is known in Gaelic, is one of the best-known landmarks in Argyll

(photograph by Gordon Ross Thomson)

Ballachulish House as it is today. The building is dated c.1764 and presumably
incorporates part of the original house, erected on the same site by
John Stewart, or 'Young Ballachulish', in 1752
(see chapter 8; photograph by Malcolm MacGregor)

The present-day Ardsheal House stands on the
south shore of Loch Linnhe *(courtesy of Neil and Philippa Sutherland)*

Soon, however, came word that Sir Duncan Campbell of Auchinbreck, foremost general of Clan Campbell, had also landed with a force from Ireland and was heading north. Montrose led his army through Appin but such was his haste that both the Campbell strongholds of Barcaldine Castle and Castle Stalker were spared from any attack.

Nonetheless, the garrisons were hungry. By December of the following year Barcaldine Castle was drained of grain and the captain of Dunstaffnage was asked to send some food. He is known to have sent meal to Sir Donald Campbell of Ardnamurchan who claimed he was in 'extreme necessitie' in Castle Stalker. [7]

The Stewarts of Appin, consistently loyal to their monarch, joined the Royalist call to arms. Duncan Mor Stewart, 8th of Appin; Duncan, 2nd of Ardsheal; and Alexander, 4th of Invernahyle, between them brought nearly 200 men to join Montrose's standard. With him, they struggled across the snow-covered mountains on his famous march from Kilcumun. In a decisive move, they settled on a position above the old fortress of Inverlochy where Argyll's army was encamped. At daybreak, on Sunday, 2 February, 1645, together with the Camerons and MacDonalds, they charged down upon the enemy and won the most spectacular victory of all of Montrose's campaign.

Following the battle, the Stewarts were given leave to go home to plant the harvest. When they re-joined Montrose in April, they were influential in his triumph at the Battle of Auldearn. Later, in August, they fought with him at Kilsyth but, following this last of his victories, they again returned home for the harvest; mercifully missing the slaughter of the Royal army in the disaster of Philiphaugh.

[7] From D. Stevenson, *Alasdair MacColla and the Highland Problem in the Seventeenth Century*, p. 216.

In 1646, Charles I surrendered to the Army of the Covenant.

The lands of both Stewart of Appin and of Invernahyle were then forfeited by the Committee of Estates, as the Scottish Parliament was called. Vindictive directions were issued for the district of Appin to be ravaged 'by fire and sword' but fortunately Stewart of Ardvorlich persuaded General Leslie to remit this dreadful punishment.

Restoration of Charles II

In 1660, when Charles II was restored as king, the Stewarts of Appin regained their attainted land. In 1682, when the Protestant 9th Earl of Argyll was opposed to the Catholic James VII and II, the Campbell prestige was low and John Stewart of Ardsheal seized the chance to raise an action for the return of Castle Stalker to his ward, Robert Stewart of Appin, who was then still a minor. In 1684, the privy council ordered John Campbell, 3rd of Airds, to restore the castle to Robert, but Campbell refused to comply. Besieged by the furious Stewarts — one hundred and twenty of them, so he claimed — he remained defiant, and when James Guthrie, Dingwall Pursuivant, appeared from Edinburgh to implement the council's orders, he was attacked by Campbell and his followers 'who fell upon and did most beatt, bruise and wound [him] and broke his trumpet'.

The Battle of Killiecrankie

27 July, 1689

The Stewarts finally retrieved the castle in 1686 but their occupation was brief for, loyal to the Jacobites, they fought at the Battle of Killiecrankie under James Graham of Claverhouse, or 'Bonnie Dundee' as he was known.

Robert Stewart, 9th of Appin, was only a boy of sixteen. He was still at university when, on Dundee's summons, he called his men to arms. On 27 July, 1689, the Stewarts of Appin, fighting beside the Camerons of Lochiel, fell upon King William's army. 'No Lowlander who fought at Killiecrankie ever wanted to see a broadsword charge again.'[8]

On 21 August, the Jacobite army attacked the town of Dunkeld. The Stewarts were led by their chief's tutor, John Stewart of Ardsheal; his brother, Alexander; James of Fasnacloich; Alexander of Ballachulish and by Robert of Appin himself, but the musket fire of the enemy overcame them and they were forced to retire.

So great were the casualties that, when a few days later, the Jacobite chiefs signed a bond to renew hostilities at an unspecified future date, the young chief of Appin could promise only 100 men.

As it turned out, however, the opportunity for renewed rebellion disappeared. Robert Stewart of Appin was forfeited and Castle Stalker was surrendered upon terms in October 1690.

[8] Michael Starforth, *Clan Stewart of Appin*, p. 36.

The Jacobite Rising of 1715

Robert Stewart of Appin's Estates Confiscated

Twenty-five years later, in August 1715, John Earl of Mar summoned the Highland chiefs to a so-called 'hunting party' at Braemar. There he put forward his plan to raise an army to put the Stewart King James VIII and III on the throne in place of the Hanoverian George I. Among those who signed a pledge to join him were the MacDonalds of Glengarry and Clanranald, MacLean of Duart, Cameron of Lochiel, the Campbell Earl of Breadalbane, MacGregor of Glengyle and, most notably, Stewart of Appin.

On 6 September, Mar raised his standard at Braemar. On the 15th, the Duke of Argyll established his headquarters in Stirling, but Mar had devised a plan which would lure him away to defend his own land in Argyll. Accordingly, General Alexander Gordon of Auchintoul, in command of the Highland force, advanced upon the little town of Inveraray. On 19 October his army encamped on the green sward at the mouth of Glen Shira, just a mile east of the town.

The men slept wrapped in their plaids, most of them on the open ground. Among them was a very excited boy; this was his first campaign. He was a short lad called James Stewart, the natural son of John Stewart of Ardsheal; the oak leaves in his bonnet depicted the badge of his clan.

Another young man, some five years older than himself, wore a sprig of pine. To James he must have seemed a hero, for this was none other than James Mor MacGregor, eldest son of the now almost legendary Rob Roy. Tall and handsome, he sat his garron with the ease of a born horseman and it was reported that he could handle a claymore with something near his father's skill. A piper almost as good as a MacCrimmon, he could stir the hearts of his clansmen when leading them to war.

Little did the two young soldiers, camped on the shores of Loch Fyne, guess how their paths would cross. Neither could imagine how the malevolence of Lord Islay, brother of the Duke of Argyll, and now holding Inveraray Castle, would one day threaten the lives of both of them.

The siege of Inveraray proved fruitless for want of heavy artillery. The castle walls stood firm. Gordon's men pillaged what they could from the surrounding farms and blockaded the passes to the north. Rob Roy's capture of a ship in Loch Fyne was the only decisive action of the campaign.

Recalled from Argyllshire in October, Gordon's division reached Auchterarder in Perthshire on 4 November. From there they joined Mar's army in Perth. On the 10th, they marched towards Stirling. Argyll advanced to meet them, and on 13 November the two forces faced each other on Sheriffmuir.

The Stewarts of Appin were on Mar's left wing. The young James Stewart, following his father, yelled his lungs out in the madness of a Highland charge. But Argyll's cavalry outflanked them and the men fell before the horses and the slashing swords of the dragoons.

James Stewart survived. So did James Mor MacGregor for the simple reason that his father, Rob Roy, refused to charge. Apologists claim that, arriving late and seeing the battle lost, he did not want to waste lives. But Rob Roy was nothing if not a realist. The battle was virtually over, so he made the most of the situation by raiding both baggage trains.

James VIII and III landed in Scotland on 22 December, 1715, to find that his cause was lost. The following February, he fled on a French ship. The Jacobite army was disbanded and Robert Stewart of Appin, his estates confiscated by the Crown, was forced to live abroad in exile for some twenty years, until his death in the mid 1730s.

The MacLarens of Balquhidder

Alliance with the Stewarts of Appin Renewed

The marriage of John Stewart, Lord of Lorn, to the daughter of MacLaren of Ardveich in 1463 had founded a long-lasting friendship between the two clans. In 1728, relations were re-established when John MacLaren married Beatrix, daughter of Stewart of Invernahyle.

John had inherited the barony of Stob Chon (the Hound's Peak), an estate beyond the head of Balquhidder, to the south-east of Loch Doine, which includes the mountain of that name. His land marched with that of Malcolm MacGregor of Marchfield, a first cousin of the now notorious Rob Roy, and laird of Inverlochlarig at the head of Loch Doine. Malcolm MacGregor, having got into debt, decided to emigrate, but got no farther than Oban when he died. He left behind a widow and a large number of children for whom Rob Roy felt himself bound to provide. The Marchfield estate was divided up and John MacLaren seized the chance to take possession of a farm called Wester Invernenty, which lay adjacent to his land. Rob Roy was openly furious – he had wanted it for a tenant of his own. He collected about a hundred of his clansmen and took possession of the place, driving the MacLarens from the farm.

John MacLaren, now incensed, appealed to his wife's relations for help and got it – the Stewarts of Appin, headed by Ardsheal, then tutor of the clan, marched in a body to his aid. Joined by the Stewarts of Glenbuckie, they gathered above the village of Kirkton in Balquhidder where Rob Roy found himself confronted with a force of at least two hundred men.

Knowing he was outnumbered, Rob Roy advanced to parley under a white flag of truce. He conceded MacLaren's right to occupy Wester Invernenty farm, but at that moment MacLaren's brother-in-law, Stewart of Invernahyle, leapt forward and challenged him to a duel.

Rob Roy was famed throughout Scotland as a swordsman but now, with his limbs growing stiff and his eyesight failing, he could not outmatch the younger man. Wounded, with blood pouring from his arm, he acknowledged defeat. Invernahyle gallantly insisted that youth alone had given him victory but Rob, throwing down his claymore, swore he would use it no more. This contest, in the autumn of 1734, proved the start of his decline. His wound never healed properly and in late December he died.

Rob Roy's widow allegedly incited her sons to gain revenge. James Mor, the eldest, was renowned as a handsome rogue with a reputation for unscrupulously exploiting anyone to further his own ends. He had great influence over his younger brother, Robin Oig, who, although his mother's favourite, was unattractive and weak-willed. In 1734, when their father died, Robin Oig was described as 'a tall lad, aged about twenty, thin, pale-coloured, squint-eyed, pock-pitted, ill-legged, in-kneed and broad-footed [with] brown hair'.[9]

Almost certainly, it was James Mor who actually plotted the assassination and forced his younger brother to kill MacLaren.

[9] *The Braes o' Balquhidder*, p. 128

A long-barrelled Spanish gun, which had belonged to their father, had just been mended by a famous gunsmith in the nearby town of Doune. With this, Robin Oig crept up behind John MacLaren while he was ploughing a field. Firing from behind, he shattered his victim's thigh with a bullet which sent him spinning forward into the furrow between the stilts of the plough. There was no doctor available and so MacLaren was attended to by a local man who probed his wound with a cabbage stalk. Not surprisingly, he died on the same night.

Robin Oig, summoned to stand trial, managed to escape to France. His brothers, James and Ronald, were not so fortunate and were arrested and brought to trial at the High Court of Justiciary on 16 July, 1736. The jury found the charges of conspiracy to murder MacLaren unproven, but both brothers 'were ordained to find caution each to the amount of £200 for their good behaviour for seven years.' [10]

[10] Dr. A. H. Millar, *Gregarach*, p 45.

CHAPTER 2

Jacobite Rising of 1745
The Men of Argyll Divided by Loyalty to King and Prince

Thirty years later, in August 1745, Prince Charles Edward landed in Moidart and the Stewarts of Appin were again called to arms. Their chief, Dugald, 10th of Appin, refused to command the Appin Regiment. The excuse, offered by the Dewar Manuscripts (a collection of legends gathered by a Gaelic-speaking forester for the 8th Duke of Argyll), that he was too young, is invalid – 'He was an adult in 1740 let alone 1745.'[1]

In fairness, he did have a good reason for refusing to fight for the Prince. His father, Robert, 9th of Appin, had died an exile abroad and his estates, forfeited in 1689 and again in 1715, had only been restored to Dugald in an act of amnesty about ten years before. So he remained in Edinburgh while Charles Stewart of Ardsheal, as hereditary tutor of the clan, commanded the Appin Regiment in his place.

Charles Stewart had, in fact, held a commission as Colonel of the Appin Regiment from James VIII and III, dated 17 May,

[1] Michael Starforth, *Clan Stewart of Appin*, p. 44

1739. A giant of a man and heavily built, he was known locally as *Tearlach Mor* and his swordsmanship was renowned throughout Scotland. In 1731, while courting Isabel Haldane of Lanrick, near Callander, he reputedly fell out with Rob Roy MacGregor during an evening's drinking in Balquhidder and defeated him in a duel.

So it was that in 1745, he led his clan to war. With him, as a company commander, went a small, stocky farmer: his tacksman in Glen Duror, James Stewart of the Glen. James, who as a boy had fought in the campaign of 1715, was now middle-aged. His sons were too young to fight, but he knew that the young man he had fostered from childhood, dubbed Allan Breck ('spotted') because of his pitted face, had enlisted in the army of King George.

From Glenfinnan, Prince Charles led his army by Invergarry Castle, over the Corrieyairack Pass and then through the Forest of Dalnacardoch to Blair Castle. On 4 September, he entered Perth where he appointed Lord George Murray and the Duke of Perth as generals of his army. Six days later he set off for Edinburgh, where, early on the morning of the 17th, the Camerons, by a clever strategy, managed to enter the city by the Netherbow port. The Stewarts of Appin and the MacGregors coming close behind were followed by the rest of the Highland army, and by evening the capital, save only for the castle, was in their hands.

On 20 September came news that a large force of the Hanoverian army, commanded by General Cope and the Earl of Loudoun, was ten miles south of Edinburgh. The Prince led his men out to meet them and slept that night at the foot of a beanstack near Port Seton, together with the Duke of Perth, MacGregor of Glencarnock and Stewart of Ardsheal.

At daybreak, the Jacobite army rose silently and surprised the enemy. The MacDonalds were on the right, their hereditary place of honour since Bannockburn. Next in line came the Drummonds, the MacGregors, the Stewarts and finally the Camerons.

A first-hand account, written by a MacGregor,[2] describes how, advancing upon the enemy to within forty or fifty yards, 'we fired and gave a loud huzza, we left our guns, drew our swords and targes like lions . . . then they broke and we hashed them and slaughtered at them like fury.'

The Duke of Perth's men 'stood like as many oxen' but the MacGregors, taking their place, fought 'in the very heat of the battle . . . James Mor MacGregor gave a great call to the MacDonalds to close in on the left.' Then he fell. A shot from a musket had broken his thigh.

Charles Stewart of Ardsheal led his men in pursuit of the Hanoverian forces as they broke and ran. Highland men seized the chance to change sides and among them was a tall knock-kneed man whose face still bore the scars of small-pox. He was none other than the foster son of James of the Glen.

The battle was a great victory for the Jacobites. A month later the Prince led his army into England, but at Derby, on 6 December (Black Friday), he learned that overwhelming forces were advancing against him. Reluctantly, he abandoned his attempt to reach London. Dispirited, like most of his men, he began the long return to Scotland.

Near Penrith, at Clifton, the rearguard of his army, which included the Stewarts of Appin, was attacked by the pursuing cavalry. Night fell and in the moonlight the Stewarts drove off their attackers and escaped almost unscathed.

The Jacobite army reached Glasgow where Ardsheal sent

[2] A.G.M. MacGregor, *History of the Clan Gregor*, pp. 367–8.

two of his commanders, Invernahyle and Fasnacloich, to Appin to raise more recruits and to round up some deserters. The Highlanders thirsted to sack the city, but Lochiel persuaded the Prince to forbid this, much to the inhabitants' relief.

On 3 January, 1746, Prince Charles advanced upon Stirling with the object of taking the castle. Some 4,000 men, who had gathered at Perth, now joined his army and, with this formidable strength, he encountered the Hanoverian force, commanded by General Hawley, at Falkirk.

Now, for the first time the men of Appin found themselves ranged against their own countrymen. Lord Glenorchy, who, unlike his father the Earl of Breadalbane, was a staunch supporter of King George II, had raised a company of Argyll militiamen. Among them was a young man from a township in upper Glenorchy. His name was Duncan MacIntyre and he was known for his fair hair as 'Duncan Ban'. Duncan was actually deputising for an old man, Fletcher of Crannach, who claimed to be too infirm to take the field. Armed with Fletcher's rusty sword, Duncan set off to war in high spirits, as the first of his poems records: '*A' dol an coinneamh a' Phrionnsa, gum bu shunndach a bha sinne*' (while going to engage the Prince, verily we were light-hearted). Alas, they were soon disillusioned, as the following translation shows.

What time the men donned their armour,
intending to head off the rebels,
we never thought, until we gave way,
that it was we who would be driven.
As when a dog would set on sheep,
and they scamper on a glen slope,
so they did suffer dispersal
on the side for which we fought.

Duncan, running for his life, dropped Fletcher's old sword. Returning to Glenorchy without it, he found himself without reward, but Lord Glenorchy intervened and forced Fletcher to pay his debt.

Colonel Jack Campbell, writing to his father, the Major-General, on 18 January, 1746, was scathing about the Argyll recruits. 'Our militia was not engag'd, but as half of them dispersed and deserted, we have been terribly fatigued.'

On the 27th, General Campbell replied, 'The bad behaviour of near half of our Argyllshire militia is in a great measure owing to the officers . . . The Lord Glenorchy and Duncan Campbell are very much vex't at some of their men and swear they shall be sent back to Dumbarton.'

Without doubt, the Jacobites had won a great victory at the Battle of Falkirk and many of the Highlanders, who had raided the surrounding district, now went home with their loot. The Prince wanted to attack the enemy again, but Lord George Murray realised that, as the castle was still held by a strong garrison while they had lost many of their army, it was too enormous a risk.

On 29 January, Murray presented the Prince with a petition signed by the Highland chiefs of his army, including Lochiel and Ardsheal. They asked to be allowed to retreat to the north where, they assured him, recruits would be found.

On 3 February, Lieutenant-General Hawley wrote to Major-General Campbell to tell him of the siege of Stirling Castle. 'The rebels are still flying,' he claimed. General Campbell had already sent seven companies of the Argyllshire militia to Dumbarton and now, with four of them, he marched north in pursuit of the rebels. On 6 February, he reached Dunblane and three days later he joined the Duke of Cumberland at Perth. He was appalled at the plundering and looting, and general ill-treatment of the Jacobite supporters (to which Cumberland was apparently turning a blind eye), and put a stop to it.

That same day, three more companies of the Argyllshire militia reached Crieff, bringing no less than 1,200 men. The difficulty of feeding so many soldiers and horses in a country already ravaged by fighting was such that, on 17 February, General Campbell, by now ill with rheumatic fever, took half of his force back to Inveraray.

The Duke of Cumberland then decided to use the men of the Argyllshire militia who remained with him (under the command of the General's son, Colonel Campbell) to man the outposts in Perthshire. A small garrison placed at the end of Loch Rannoch was commanded by Colin Campbell of Glenure, a lieutenant in the Earl of Loudoun's regiment. He was a red-headed young man who had fought valiantly under General Campbell at Fontenoy, thus earning regard. Colin was specifically ordered to stop Jacobites escaping across the Moor of Rannoch in their attempt to get home.

Prince Charles's army retreated north to Inverness which was held by the Earl of Loudoun and MacLeod of MacLeod. Warned of the approaching force, they decided to evacuate the city almost as the vanguard of Prince Charles's army entered its gates. The garrison of Inverness Castle surrendered after a short siege and the building was largely destroyed. The Stewarts of Appin, commanded by Ardsheal, stayed at what had become the Prince's headquarters in Inverness. Two of the cadet chiefs, Invernahyle and young Fasnacloich, however, returned to Appin to raise more recruits.

On 20 February, Fort George was seized by the Jacobites.

An attack on Maryburgh, the old town which surrounded the barracks of Fort William, then seemed imminent and a band of militia was sent forthwith to reinforce the garrison of Castle Stalker. However, on the news of Prince Charles's landing, the Duke of Argyll had despatched a sergeant with twelve men to hold the castle. The militia garrison, which replaced them on 12 February, 1746, was commanded by Donald Campbell of Octomore, an elderly officer from Islay. His main task was to protect the military stores within the great cellars and to transmit the intelligence for which government ships from Fort William called every other day.

On 27 February, Cumberland wrote to General Campbell to inform him that, 'As it is not impossible but the hasty surrender of Fort George may encourage the rebels . . . I have thought fit to send Captain Caroline Frederick Scott, who will be the bearer of this, to you, to take command of Fort William . . . you will therefore assist him with your advice, and to the utmost of your power . . . particularly that you may furnish him with such a number of men, as he may think necessary for the reinforcement of the garrison.'[3]

[3] Sir James Fergusson, *Argyll in the Forty-Five*, p. 101.

Captain Scott left Inveraray and rode to Dunstaffnage via the ferry which crossed Loch Awe from Portsonachan to Taycreggan. From Dunstaffnage he headed north to Castle Stalker. On 10 March, he wrote to General Campbell to tell him that he had collected all the axes from the local people both on the mainland and on the island of Lismore.

Because of the threat of an ambush, soldiers from Fort William had already destroyed the houses round the landing points of the Corran Ferry on both sides of Loch Linnhe. Several supposedly dangerous men had been killed. Nonetheless, the tracks through the wooded slopes along the shore were still unsafe and so Captain Caroline Scott waited at Castle Stalker until a well-armed wherry, the *Victory* arrived to carry him on to Fort William by sea. His good sense in taking this precaution was proved some six years later when another traveller, this time coming from Fort William along the wooded road by the shore, was killed by a lurking assassin with a gun.

Scott, however, reached Fort William safely on 13 March. He arrived just in time to organise the town's defence before the Jacobites attacked.

Meanwhile, in Perthshire, Lord George Murray, who had marched south from the Prince's headquarters in Inverness, achieved a sudden victory in what has since been called the Atholl Raid. He took two of the outposts manned by the Argyllshire militia, who were all killed or taken prisoner. It soon transpired that both of the Campbell commanders had been absent from their posts. One was Campbell of Knockbuy, the other Colin Campbell of Glenure. The former was with Colonel Stewart at the Bridge of Tay, and Glenure's excuse was that he had gone to look for food for his soldiers. Returning, he had spent a night at Taymouth where his half-brother, Campbell of Barcaldine, was laid up with the gout.

General Campbell was furious. 'I received a very melancholy account of the behaviour of some of the out commands mostly belonging to the Argyllshire levies under the Earl of Loudoun's command in Perthshire. It is plain the officers are to blame, and I make no doubt that H.R.H. will order them to be tryed for their misconduct. Campbell of Glenure and Campbell of Knockbuy have the King's Commission . . . both of them absent from their commands . . . I would fain hope the conduct of the officers has not been so bad as they represented to me, if it has I hope they will be punish'd as they deserve.'[4]

The two young men were threatened with arrest but both somehow escaped punishment. Glenure then saved his reputation by becoming aid-de-camp to Lieutenant-General the Earl of Loudoun, to whom he became invaluable as a Gaelic translator.

The siege of Fort William began on 19 March, 1746, and ended with victory for the Hanoverian defenders on 3 April.

Some of the Stewarts of Appin had taken part in the siege but most of the new recruits, under the leadership of Invernahyle and young Fasnacloich, had already reached Inverness during the last week of March. From the city they marched to confront the approaching enemy on Culloden Moor. Lord George Murray had requested Prince Charles for the men of the Appin regiment to be placed on the extreme right of the line. Next to them stood the Camerons and the Stewarts of Appin, clans who were neighbours at home.

Sleet, driven by a high wind, lashed against their faces as they waited for the order to charge. At last it came and the

[4] Fergusson, p. 152.

huge figure of Charles Stewart of Ardsheal ran forward at the head of his men. Close to him, according to legend, was the pock-marked Allan Breck Stewart, who, they say, was always at his side. Miraculously, perhaps thanks to his strength and swordsmanship, Charles survived. So, too, did his half-brother, James of the Glen, and the latter's foster-son, Allan Breck.

Charles's uncle, Duncan Stewart, was not so fortunate and was among eight of his relations who were killed. Other deaths included Alexander Stewart, brother of Achnacone, and Donald Stewart, nephew of Invernahyle. In total, sixty-nine men of the Appin regiment lost their lives that day. Most lie buried in a common grave. Another sixty-five were wounded, many by the vicious grape-shot which followed the cannonade. From the records it seems that few families from Appin – not only Stewarts, but MacColls, MacLarens, Carmichaels and Livingstones – did not have men either killed or maimed on that terrible day of 16 April, 1746. [5]

[5] Michael Starforth, *Clan Stewart of Appin*, pp. 84–5.

CHAPTER 3

The Men Who Took to the Hills

Charles Stewart of Ardsheal returned from Culloden a hunted and a ruined man. After the fighting, which was done on foot, he mounted his great grey horse, MacPhail, and rode home. On reaching its swathe of green land by Loch Linnhe, he at once ordered that everything of value must be buried or hidden. His children, stripped of their own clothes and dressed in the homespun garments that the local children wore, were placed in the care of a family called MacCorquodale, who lived in one of the low-built, thatched black houses in the township of Lettermore.

At the start of the campaign, Ardsheal had entrusted the care of his family and business to the man he most trusted – his half-brother James of the Glen. Most importantly, James was in charge of the provision store in Glen Creran where he also brewed ale and distilled whisky. Now he took on the remainder of his chief's responsibilities as Ardsheal fled to the hills. Together with other Appin lairds, Charles hid in a cave in remote Glenstockdale.

Isabel, his wife, remained at Ardsheal House. In May,

government soldiers appeared and drove away the cattle but General Campbell specifically ordered the milk cows to be returned. He wrote to Isabel Stewart.

Madam, your misfortune and the unhappy situation Ardsheal has brought you and your innocent children into, by being so deeply concerned at this unjust and unnatural rebellion, makes my hear ache . . . I have taken the liberty of ordering back your milk cows, six weathers, and as many lambs; the men who pretend a right to them shall be paid. I have taken the freedom at the same time of ordering two bolls of meal, out of my stores, to be left here for you, which I desire you to accept to the use of yourself and your little ones.

Thus, for the time being, Ardsheal's wife and family were saved from starvation. In November, however, the dreaded Redcoats returned and this time their officer was none other than Captain Caroline Scott. Notorious for his cruelty to the Jacobites, Scott ordered his soldiers to destroy everything they could find. Nothing was spared, to the point where even the fruit trees were cut down. Ardsheal House was set on fire and Isabel fled to a barn where that very night, according to tradition, she gave birth to Anne, her last child. Ardsheal, in his place of hiding, saw flames and smoke in the sky and guessed what had happened.

Captain Scott is supposed to have come to see Isabel and found her with her new-born baby lying upon straw in the barn. When he left, he must have exchanged words with the guard, allowing Isabel to hear that the cave in Glen Stockdale had been discovered and men were already on their way to capture the fugitives within. Frantic to save her husband, she managed to send a fleet highlander named Buchanan to outrun the soldiers over the hills. Arriving, they found an empty cave. Ardsheal had escaped.

He found refuge in the cave of *Eas nan Con*, by a waterfall in the burn which plunges down the steep, north-facing slope of *Beinn a Bheithir*, above the farm of Lagnaha. His wife managed to send him food and some of their home-brewed ale, and perhaps brandy as well.

Eventually, however, one of his own men succumbed to a bribe to betray him and Captain Scott came from Fort William

The waterfall above Lagnaha. The cave below is where Charles Stewart of Ardsheal hid in 1746. Folklore has it that it was from here that he saw the smoke rising above the hill and knew that his home had been set alight.

with no less than sixty men. But Ardsheal had been warned of their approach – they had crossed the narrows of Loch Leven by the ferry – and he mounted his trusty MacPhail. He was nearly caught in Glen Duror. Hiding behind a rock, he heard soldiers clattering by on the track. Quickly, he continued upwards, hidden by mist. But, as he crossed the watershed into Glen Creran, a shaft of sunlight burst through the clouds and the great grey horse was seen.

MacPhail, now tiring with the weight of his rider, was sinking into boggy ground. Dismounting, Charles struggled on, thanks to the help of his men who propelled him onwards with a plank of wood, two of them at either end. By this means he managed to reach Glen Etive where a farmer is supposed to have hidden him in a kiln used for drying corn while the Redcoats searched in vain.

From Glen Etive, after more adventures, he eventually reached Leith. There, in the guise of a wine merchant, he managed to board a ship. Sailing across the North Sea he reached Flanders and shortly crossed the border into France. His brave Isabel joined him in 1749.

CHAPTER 4

The Farmer called Seumas a' Ghlinne

C harles left his home secure in the knowledge that his half-brother James, then the tacksman of Glen Duror and known by the Gaelic-speaking people of the district as *Seumas a' Ghlinne*, would continue to look after his affairs.

Both men were sons of John Stewart, 4th of Ardsheal, but Seumas (or James) was his natural son and was the elder of the two. James was born in the early years of the eighteenth century, probably about 1702. Scotland then had its own parliament and he must have been about five years old when the Treaty of Union was signed at Loudoun Castle in Ayrshire in 1707.

He described himself as 'a schoolboy' at the time of the Jacobite Rising of 1715, 'and little more in the year 1719' when George Keith, the Earl Marischal of Scotland, sailed from Spain to join forces with Lord Tullibardine in what proved to be another futile attempt to put James VIII on the throne.

As the son of John Stewart of Ardsheal, James was granted a

tack, or lease, of Glen Duror, the long, winding glen, now largely forested, which runs from high ground to low-lying fields before reaching Loch Linnhe at Cuil Bay. In taking his farm, James bound himself to the usual obligation of a tacksman, namely to lead the men who lived and worked on his land to fight for his chief, Stewart of Appin, when summoned in time of war. So, when his half-brother Charles, deputising for their chief, Dugald Stewart of Appin, commanded the Appin Regiment in 1745, James also raised a company of men. So many were killed in action that when peace was restored, he introduced new tenants on to Ardsheal's – by then forfeited – land.

Following the legislation of 1746, which ended heritable jurisdiction and the right of a chief to raise an army, the tacksmen lost their military status and had to improve their farms to meet ever-increasing rents. James had seen many changes in the course of his half century but none of them more drastic than those which were now taking place.

In his youth, the common practice had been to kill the majority of the small, black-and-brown cattle in November because of the lack of winter feed. The carcasses, salted down in tubs, had been the mainstay of Highland homes. Later, the introduction of turnips proved to be a milestone, allowing beasts to survive the winter, and an even greater innovation was the common planting of potatoes, which thrive in almost any soil. By the 1750s, potatoes had become a staple diet for people whose living depended on the land. This was largely because cattle had become so valuable on the hoof. James was a cattle-dealer on what seems to have been a large scale. His business was increasing to the point where he found it economical to rent extra ground for his herds. These animals, having been fattened, were then driven in the autumn to the markets in central Scotland where they found a ready sale.

James had a great knowledge of the land and was known as a good judge of beasts. Weather-beaten and bow-legged from many hours astride a horse, he was a kenspeckle figure to whom people deferred. A practical, rather than a 'gentleman', farmer, as were some of his kind, he was up at an early hour and worked until the light faded, directing and supervising his men. Now past middle age, he was probably affected by the rheumatism which was so indigenous to the Highlands, and he was often to be seen sitting on a rock, watching his men working while easing his weary frame.

The lives of most people in the West Highlands, as in most other agricultural communities in Scotland during the eighteenth century, were dominated by sheer hard work. Existence largely depended on what the soil could produce. Ploughing was done with a team of horses with a man walking backwards in front to guide them but much of the soil was turned over by hand with the *caschrom*, as the long, pointed spade was called. The cottars, or small tenants, who had a few beasts of their own, worked part-time for the farmer, in lieu of a bit of land for cropping and grazing for their animals. They also herded the laird's cattle with their own on the high pasture in the hills. There were very few enclosures and in summer the cows had to be driven to the mountains to keep them off the planted ground and places where a hay crop could be grown. The women and children who drove them and herded them on the *airidhs*, or high pastures, slept in the rough stone huts, which can be traced as ruins today. Most are near handy supplies of water, such as lochs and burns, and butter was preserved in peat bogs, refrigerators of the time.

Peat-cutting was another summer job and women's work was endless, summer and winter alike. Water had to carried in and emptied out, the cows milked, and wool spun and woven to make cloth. Most of the material for the plaids worn by both men and women, and used for domestic items such as blankets, was woven at home. Lengths of tartan material, which were made into kilt and plaid, were now kept in the kists, the wooden chests that held most of the family possessions. The wearing of Highland dress, prohibited in 1746, meant that the men folk had to wear Lowland garb. '*S O tha a'bhriogais liathghlas, Am bliadhna cur mulaid oirmm!*' (Oh the light-grey breeches, cast a gloom on us this year!), bewailed Duncan Ban MacIntyre, the poet of Glenorchy.

James Stewart's house at Acharn c.1900; the original thatched roof by then replaced with galvanised iron

Clothes like these were usually made by one of the local tailors who lived in the farming township. The coat with the 'silver' buttons, which Allan Breck was to borrow, being a case in point.

Few men, other than the lairds and the ministers, could either read or write. Women were valued for their efficiency as housewives and dairymaids, not for the intelligence they possessed. It was actually thought dangerous to teach them to write – they might try to communicate with men!

James's wife, Margaret (sister of William Stewart the merchant of Maryburgh), seems to have been a good manager for all that she was illiterate. The barefooted girls and men servants who worked in the house obviously treated her with respect. Her husband, good-natured as he was, appears to have been under her thumb. She certainly knew how to cope with him when he was the worse for drink.

James of the Glen was not alone in this respect. The Highlanders of those days were very much addicted to their dram, and James was both a distiller of whisky and a brewer of ale. 'The right of malt and brewstery,' was a common perquisite on most Highland estates. One advantage of leaving his original house at Achindarroch for the smaller one at Acharn,[1] further down Glen Duror, was that the brew house was near the house. His long-barrelled sporting gun was kept there as the door was always locked.

The store of Glen Duror, which provided vital income to the Ardsheal estate sold household necessities such as salt and fine flour, needles, linen thread, iron pots for cooking, and leeches to ease headaches, as well as various other things which could not be made at home. Charles of Ardsheal's main wholesaler was the merchant known as the *muileartach* (miller)

[1] See page 67.

in Leith and it is probable that James continued to deal with him. This may also be the reason why he stayed so long in Edinburgh in April 1752.

We do not know whether all Isabel Stewart's children went with her in 1749, when she went to join her exiled husband in France. Presumably, she took the youngest daughter, Anne, who cannot have been more than three years old, but she may have left the older ones with the family called MacCorquodale, with whom they had been lodged when their father went into hiding after Culloden.

The welfare of Ardsheal's children was one of the main reasons why James was so deeply concerned over the proposed eviction of the tenants. These people, poor as they were, managed by some means to pay a double rent – one to the crown, their landlord; the other to the family of their banished laird. Their generosity, remarkable as it may seem, proves the traditional loyalty of the clans people to their chief. James is believed to have sent gold to Charles and Isabel in France. The money was probably conveyed by his foster-son, the man known as Allan Breck, who, having reached France after Culloden to join the French army, was now a secret agent for the Jacobite cause.

James's fealty to his half-brother must have set the latter's mind at rest in that, apart from receiving the necessary income, he knew that his interests at home remained in the safest of hands. The responsibility thrust upon James, however, placed him in an invidious position – as a leading figure in Appin, deputising for Ardsheal, and a known Jacobite, he was believed to be a danger to the Hanoverian regime.

Rumours that Prince Charles would attempt another invasion, backed by a French force, were rife throughout the

Highlands and the Isles. With Ardsheal in France and the chief, Dugald Stewart of Appin, held in little respect, James of the Glen, commander of a company in the Rising of seven years before, was regarded as a man of authority among people still largely believed to be rebels, despite the fact that most of them had sworn allegiance to King George.

Campbells of Barcaldine & Glenure

~ family tree ~

SIR DUNCAN CAMPBELL, 7th of Glenorchy

PATRICK (Para Dubh Beag), b.1592

natural son of above, legitimised under the Court of the Great Seal of Scotland, 27 Dec. 1614

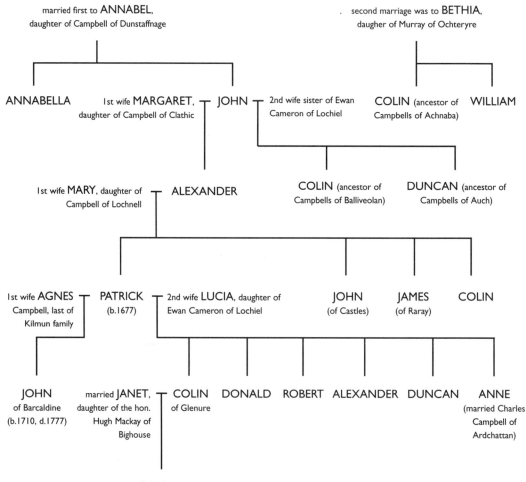

married first to ANNABEL,
daughter of Campbell of Dunstaffnage

second marriage was to BETHIA,
daugher of Murray of Ochteryre

ANNABELLA

1st wife MARGARET,
daughter of Campbell of Clathic

JOHN

2nd wife sister of Ewan
Cameron of Lochiel

COLIN (ancestor of
Campbells of Achnaba)

WILLIAM

1st wife MARY, daughter of
Campbell of Lochnell

ALEXANDER

COLIN (ancestor of
Campbells of Balliveolan)

DUNCAN (ancestor of
Campbells of Auch)

1st wife AGNES
Campbell, last of
Kilmun family

PATRICK
(b.1677)

2nd wife LUCIA, daughter of
Ewan Cameron of Lochiel

JOHN
(of Castles)

JAMES
(of Raray)

COLIN

JOHN
of Barcaldine
(b.1710, d.1777)

married JANET,
daughter of the hon.
Hugh Mackay of
Bighouse

COLIN
of Glenure

DONALD

ROBERT

ALEXANDER

DUNCAN

ANNE
(married Charles
Campbell of
Ardchattan)

3 daughters

CHAPTER 5

Forfeiture of the Jacobite Estates

F ollowing the suppression of the Rising of 1745, the estates of the Jacobites who were attainted as traitors were administered by the Barons of Exchequer. This government office, consisting of four Barons presided over by a Chief Baron, succeeded the Baron's Court. Under its auspices the forfeited lands were surveyed and factors appointed as administrators with authority to lift the rents.

In Argyll, Lord Glenorchy (later the 3rd Earl of Breadalbane) advised the appointment of two of his distant cousins as factors – John Campbell of Barcaldine and his half-brother, Colin of Glenure. The family estate of Barcaldine had gone to John, son of their father's first marriage, and Glenure had been given to Colin, eldest son of his second marriage to Lucia, daughter of Sir Ewan Cameron of Lochiel.

Colin Campbell was known as *Cailean Ruadh* (Red Colin) on account of the colour of his hair and was, by contemporary accounts, a most likeable and good-looking young man. Nonetheless, the fact that his mother was a Cameron, sister of Donald Cameron of Lochiel, was enough to throw suspicion on his name. Thought to be in sympathy with the Jacobites, his absence from the outpost in Blair Atholl, when it was captured in February 1746, was taken, at least by some, as proof of where his loyalty lay.

Glenure was not at Culloden, but accusations that he named some of the prisoners afterwards may carry some truth. While in Aberdeen, he wrote a letter to his half-brother Barcaldine, dated 21 April, 1746. Having described what he called 'a compleat victory', he tells him that 'numbers of prisoners are brought here every moment'.[1] It does, therefore, seem likely that he was called upon to identify men and, being under suspicion, he may have done so to clear his name.

The wisdom of Lord Glenorchy in influencing Colin's appointment as factor of the Cameron estates of Mamore and Callart was considered questionable, but Glenorchy refused to change his mind. Furthermore, Colin was given charge of the much smaller estate of the exiled Charles Stewart of Ardsheal.

Ardsheal was in fact the only laird in Appin to be attainted. The lairds of Ballachulish, Fasnacloich, Achnacone and Invernahyle all 'qualified to the government', that is, they swore loyalty to the King. Stewart of Appin was spared because he had refused to rise for Prince Charles, and thus Ardsheal, who had commanded the Appin regiment in his place, paid the price of loyalty to the Jacobite cause.

The Commission by the Barons of his Majesty's Exchequer to Colin Campbell of Glenure to be factor of the lands and estates of Charles Stewart of Ardsheal was issued on 3 February, 1749. In fact, he had been acting in that capacity for several months, as is proved by his previous instructions to James Stewart of the Glen to warn the Ardsheal tenants to have their rents ready for collection.

[1] *Notable Scottish Trials*, edited by D. N. Mackay, p. 303.

Barcaldine Castle, Benderloch, one of the castles built by Sir Duncan Campbell, 7th of Glenorchy, also known as 'Black Duncan of the Cowl'. Standing on a low ridge near the south shore of Loch Creran, when it was finished in 1609, it was the largest building in the area

(photograph by Malcolm MacGregor)

Glenure House is one of the best examples of an Argyllshire eighteenth-century house and is much as it was when it was built by Colin Campbell
(photograph by Roy Summers)

Boinne na Gibbet (Rock of the Gibbet) on the far side of the narrows under Ballachulish Bridge where the gallows were thrown into the water

Like most people in the neighbourhood, Glenure had a great respect for *Seumas a' Ghlinne*, as he was generally known, and they enjoyed 'a very good friendship'[2] at this time. Glenure, therefore, made the sensible decision of asking James to act as his under-factor.

In 1740, shortly after acquiring his estate, Colin Campbell of Glenure built a house on his land on the south-east side of Glen Creran, just below the entrance to Glenure. After leaving the army, he furnished it for, as a man of some substance, he had become betrothed. Colin was in his early forties and his intended wife was a girl of eighteen. Nonetheless, she had shown herself to be of strong character and her connections were propitious for a man of ambition. Janet Mackay was the eldest daughter of the Honourable Hugh Mackay of Bighouse and, more importantly, a niece of Lord Reay, a prominent Whig and staunch supporter of King George II.

The marriage took place on 9 May, 1749, shortly after Colin's appointment as Crown factor, and he and his wife moved into their new home. Glenure House is one of the best examples of a mid-eighteenth-century house in Argyll and is much as it was in their day. The first-floor bedrooms retain their low ceilings and the original pine panelling, and the windows remain the same size. The drawing-room was located on the ground floor, unusual in Scotland, as was the dining-room. The Campbells loved entertaining in their elegant new house to the point where a new kitchen, built at right angles to the south-west side of the house, had to be added in 1751.

Two daughters, Elizabeth and Lucy, were born to them within two years and Janet was again pregnant, with what proved to be her third daughter, in the spring of 1752. Their happiness seemed to be complete but Colin, as Crown factor,

[2] Ibid, pp. 6–7.

was increasingly under pressure. His position was unenviable. The local lairds, his neighbours, called him a traitor to the Camerons (his mother's people), while government officials thought him in sympathy with the Jacobites. His every move was watched. There were plenty people waiting to seize a chance to report him of playing a double game.

Claims were put forward that many of Lochiel's farms were let to Jacobites who paid less rent than they had done before. It was even asserted that in some cases men loyal to the King were actually turned out of their holdings in favour of Cameron of Fassifern's Jacobite friends. Fassifern, a brother of Lochiel, had not been involved in the Rising and these allegations were based entirely upon the fact that Glenure had let a farm to him simply because he offered the highest rent.

Nonetheless, bad news travels fast and rumours of Glenure's supposed duplicity soon reached the ears of the Prime Minister and the King.[3] Glenorchy stoutly defended him but, despite this, the Barons sent an order to Glenure that 'on no condition whatever was he to let a farm on a confiscated estate to any of the friends of the forfeiting Personne.'

This put Glenure in a predicament because James of the Glen came within the proscribed category, being a half-brother of Ardsheal. The two men talked the matter through. Glenure dared not disobey his orders, as James very well knew. He was also aware that Glenure was under pressure from a member of his own family who wanted Glen Duror for himself.

This was Campbell of Ballieveolan (now Drimavuich at the head of Loch Creran), a cousin of Glenure's; he wanted the tenancy of Glen Duror as the land was better than his own. James knew, like most other people in the neighbourhood, that Ballieveolan had offered a higher rent. James's son, Allan,

[3] Ibid, p. 7.

writing to Stewart of Glenbuckie, on 1 April, 1751, told him 'However it shall be a dear glen to them [before] they shall have it.'[4] It is easy to see how these words, referring to the rent, were later construed to be a murder threat.

Eventually – thanks, it would seem, to their old friendship and to James's good sense – a compromise was reached. In 1751, before the May term, James gave up his farm and his house of Achindarroch in Glen Duror, but was allowed to keep the small farm of Lettermore on the forfeited Ardsheal estate. He also took the farm of Acharn, at the mouth of Glen Duror, from the local laird, Campbell of Airds. This man, his friend and neighbour, regarded him so highly that he actually removed the existing tenant to let James have Acharn.[5] The bargain was made on the condition that part of the increased rent for Glen Duror would be passed on to the children of the exiled Charles Stewart of Ardsheal, for whom it was James's responsibility to provide.

So, for the best of reasons, did the tacksman of Glen Duror agree to leave his inheritance, proving himself above everything, a loyal and honourable man.

Despite his son Allan's antagonism to the Campbells, James himself is supposed to have remained on good terms with both Glenure and Ballieveolan although, if one of the later witnesses is to be believed, this may be in some doubt. According to one of James's servants (a man named Dugald MacColl), the two Campbells, together with James, his uncle (Stewart of Ardnamurchan), and John Stewart ('younger of Ballachulish'), saw in the New Year of 1752 'in the house of John Breck Maccombie, change-keeper [inn-keeper] at Kintalline'.[6]

Mrs James Stewart, knowing how much they would drink, wisely sent Dugald MacColl to bring her husband home.

[4] Ibid, p. 8.

[5] *Transactions of the Gaelic Society of Inverness*, vol. XXXV, p. 345.

[6] *Notable Scottish Trials*, edited by D. N. Mackay, p. 9 and pp. 165–6.

Dugald arrived to hear a loud argument going on in English, which he could not understand. Nonetheless, obedient to his mistress's orders, he marched in and, with the help of the inn-keeper and various others, carried James and his uncle, by now very drunk, out into the night air.

Both protested loudly, but (providentially as it turned out) young Ballachulish told them 'that they must not go back and that they ought to be good friends: upon which James would not stir from the place, till he was told by Glenure if he would go to his house the next day.'

Young Ballachulish went back into the inn, where, as he later testified, he found Glenure with a hanger – a dagger – in his hand. He managed to make him promise to dine with James at Acharn the next day, and when he was told this James reluctantly agreed to go home.

Dugald MacColl and a man called MacCorquodale had to carry James over the burn which ran by the inn. MacColl and John Maccombie (who was either the son or the grandson of the inn-keeper) and some others then accompanied James and his uncle back to Acharn. Unfortunately, Maccombie mentioned that young Ballachulish had told him of Glenure's drawn hanger in the room they had just left, whereupon James, now very truculent, demanded to go back to see if this was true. The men tried to argue with him but were told to mind their own business. Fortunately, however, both he and his uncle were so fuddled that, between them, Dugald and a herd-boy managed to get them back to Acharn.

Whatever the truth of this story (the witnesses are known to have lied), Glenure and Ballieveolan did dine with James and Margaret Stewart in their house the next day. It was New Year's Day and, as they raised their glasses to pledge each other's health, none of them could have guessed for a moment what lay ahead in the year to come.

James of the Glen, as the sub-factor, continued to collect the rents on Ardsheal's forfeited estate. The tenants, all small farmers, or 'cotters', were up to date with their rent, part of which went to Ardsheal's children, a fact which none seemed to grudge.

Suddenly, however, in compliance with his orders, Glenure announced that they must go. The only compromise he dared to make was to let some of them remain as 'boumen', or cattle-men, for the new tenants. James was openly furious. The eviction of poor, hard-working men, who had done nothing to deserve it, was grossly unjust. He voiced his anger to the MacColls – Dugald, John Mor and John Beg (Big John and Little John) – as he drew off the first potion of *aqua vitae*, or whisky, in the brew house and then, as was customary, handed them each a dram.

The first draw is always very potent and it certainly loosened their tongues. At his trial, James declared that he could not remember what he had said, which was probably only too true, but the MacColls, giving evidence for the prosecution, claimed he had told them, 'if Glenure went on the same way, it was likely he would in five years be laird of Appin.' The MacColls had agreed that 'this was likely to happen' whereupon James apparently retorted that 'he knew commoners once in Appin who would not allow Glenure to go on at such a rate.' [7] Ranting on under the influence of drink, the MacColls maintained he had accused the Appin men of cowardice, of lacking the courage possessed by men he had known as a boy.

Doubtless, James of the Glen was voicing worries which

[7] From the evidence of John Mor MacColl; *Notable Scottish Trials*, p. 162.

must have lain very heavy on his mind. Things were bad enough but then, at the beginning of February, who should arrive on his doorstep but his foster-son, Allan Breck, who, since his desertion from the Hanoverian army, was now a wanted man.

No one who knew him seems to have had any affection for this mysterious individual. His father was Donald Stewart, a distant cousin of James of the Glen. His mother lived in Rannoch but seems to have taken little responsibility for her son. James had taken him in and reared him with his own three young children: Allan, Charles and Elizabeth. As a child, James's foster-son had caught the then common disease of smallpox and thereafter was dubbed 'Allan Breck' (the Gaelic word *breac* means spotted or pitted). He appears to have been a difficult adolescent. Soon he was borrowing money from James to pay for drink and to cover his debts. The Stewart family must have been thankful when he went off to enlist in the Hanoverian army.

Years passed and then James of the Glen found himself fighting against his foster-son at the Battle of Prestonpans, after which Allan Breck deserted to join the army of Prince Charles. Then, after the Battle of Culloden, Allan had saved the life of James's half-brother and helped him to escape to France, so James felt himself under an obligation to help Breck when he landed once again at his door, however he misbehaved.

Following the defeat of the Jacobite army, Breck had also fled to France, where he enlisted in the army of the French king. He returned to Scotland as a spy and as a salesman of weapons to disaffected men.

Wanted man though he was, Breck now came swaggering into Appin resplendent in the uniform of a French soldier –

blue coat and breeches, red vest and cockaded hat. A tall, strapping fellow, he wore his long black hair in a queue or what was called a 'net'.

For a time he amused himself by shooting blackcock, having borrowed James's two guns. It was late March and the birds were lecking;[8] but both weapons were notoriously inaccurate and continuously misfired. Bored with this occupation, he took himself to Kentallen and the local inn where he boasted of his adventures, telling tales which were probably widely exaggerated, even untrue. Nevertheless, the local young men, who had never left Argyll, let alone Scotland, hung upon his every word.

It seemed that Breck had come to cause trouble when James of the Glen needed it least. His drinking, his raffishness and, above all, his persuasive tongue, threatened disaster. Duncan Campbell, the inn-keeper at Annat, remembered only too clearly that Breck, on one occasion, had sworn that 'he hated all of the name of Campbell' and that later, by this time very drunk, he had told Campbell to 'warn his friends that if they tried to turn out the possessors of Ardsheal's estate, he would make blackcocks of them before they entered into possession'. Campbell understood that he meant to shoot them, 'it being a common phrase in the country'.[9]

The conversation went from bad to worse. When Breck's drinking companion, John Stewart of the nearby estate of Achnacon, said that he 'did not blame Glenure so much as Ballieveolan for taking these possessions . . . Glenure was doing the King's service', Allan Breck replied that he had 'another ground of quarrel against Glenure'. Apparently, this was 'for writing to Colonel Crawford[10] that he [Breck] had come home from France'. Then, with typical bravado, Breck claimed that

[8] The time when birds gather and fan their tails in a mating dance.

[9] From the evidence of Duncan Campbell, *Notable Scottish Trials*, pp. 139–40.

[10] Who was in command of the garrison at Fort William.

he 'was too cunning for him, for that, when at Edinburgh, he had made up his peace with General Churchill, and had got his pass, which he had in his pocket-book'. When the inn-keeper asked to see it, Allan Breck simply tore a leaf out of the book and claimed that this was it.

Later, after even more alcohol, Breck again repeated that he 'would be fit-sides [a good match] with Glenure whenever he met him, and wanted nothing more than to meet him at a convenient place'.

The little thatched inn at Portnacroish was another of Breck's haunts. Later, in the witness box, its landlord, Malcolm MacColl, told a similar tale. Allan Breck was there, again with John Stewart of Achnacon, when Malcolm's servant, a man called John MacColl, came in. Breck asked who he was and John Stewart told him that 'he was an honest poor man with a numerous family of small children,' whereupon Breck asked John Stewart to give him 'a stone of meal and he would pay for it', which John promised to do. Breck then bought John MacColl a dram and reputedly told him that, 'if he would fetch him the red fox's skin he would give him what was much better'.

This could have been an innocent remark. Breck may simply have wanted a fox's pelt. Nonetheless, it was later construed to mean that he was asking the man to kill Glenure; the 'red' referring to Glenure's red hair.

On 3 April, 1752, James of the Glen set out for Edinburgh. He had business of his own to attend to and he also hoped to find legal support against the eviction of the small farmers or cotters from the Ardsheal estate. Hardly was his back turned before his foster-son was stirring things up.

Dugald and John Mor MacColl, who had been harrowing

the tath-field[11] at Acharn, were just 'loosing their horses' when Allan Breck came strolling along. At the trial, the brothers claimed to remember every word that was said during the ensuing conversation. Dugald reported that Breck began by telling them about France, where so many Jacobites were now refugees. John Mor said he wished that none had ever come from that country (implying Prince Charles) and Breck agreed, saying that the Rising 'had dispersed the friends he most regarded'. He added that 'it was a particular misfortune that the management of any concerns they left behind them fell into the hands of one that was about to show them no manner of favour; and declared he meant Glenure; and told that the commoners of Appin were little worth when they did not take him out of the way before now.' When the brothers replied that 'nobody would run that risk, not knowing who would stand by them,' Breck assured them that he 'knew a way to convey out of the way any person that would do so, in a way that he would never be caught; and added that they and the tribe they were of [the MacColls] were not like to be the least sufferers by Glenure's proceedings.'[12]

[11] A manured field.

[12] From the evidence of Dugald MacColl at the trial of James Stewart of Acharn; *Notable Scottish Trials*, p. 166.

CHAPTER 6

James of the Glen's Attempt to Save the Tenants of Ardsheal

Meanwhile, James of the Glen was making his way to Edinburgh. The most direct route was through Glencoe where the military road, linking Stirling to Fort William, was nearing completion. He is known to have stopped at Tayinluib in the morning 'to have his horse corn'd' as the landlord, Alexander Campbell, afterwards deponed. He also got himself a dram.

Unfortunately, a young man called Colin MacLaren, a merchant from Stirling, who had stayed at the inn the night before, joined him and James, glad of the company, over indulged. MacLaren reputedly asked him if he would help the Campbell landlord to a dram, whereupon James supposedly retorted that 'he did but know any thing that he would help Campbell (the deponent) or any of his name to, if it was not to the gibbet.'

Campbell claimed to have protested at this, saying that 'that was not a very comfortable expression to him [and] that it seems that if any of them were at the gibbet, the panel [James] would draw down their feet.' To which James replied that 'of some of them he would, and some of them he would not'. The landlord supposed that James had the greatest quarrel with Glenure, although, as he told James, 'he did not know any good cause for it'. James retorted that if Glenure had used the landlord 'as ill as he had used him, by turning him out of his possession, he would have no less quarrel with him than he had'.

'That was no just cause of quarrel,' retorted the landlord, for if James 'had a tack of his farm, Glenure could not turn him out.'[1]

James's reply to this is not recorded. Perhaps he refused to say more.

Later, when the merchant MacLaren was asked for his version of events, he confirmed that James had refused to give the landlord a dram and that the two of them had fallen out over the justice of the Ardsheal tenants being evicted from their farms. He admitted, however, that 'having no concern in the matter, he took little notice as to what passed'.

As the merchant lived in Stirling, he accompanied James on his way up the hill to the watershed and then down through Glen Ogle. At Lochearnhead, they stopped at another tavern where the landlord, Ewan Murray, served them with further drams.

When it was his turn in the witness stand, Murray claimed to remember James telling him that 'Glenure had warned away several families in Ardsheal's estate to remove; [but] he was informed that none of the factors on the forfeited estates had power to remove the tenants.'[2] James went on to explain that he was on his way to Edinburgh 'to take advice of lawyers about it' and if he could not prove that the factor was acting

[1] From the evidence of Alexander Campbell, *Notable Scottish Trials*, p. 159.

[2] From the evidence of Ewan Murray, Ibid, p. 160.

illegally, then he would ask for a suspension of evictions of behalf of himself and the other tenants.

Apparently, James also told Murray of how he had challenged Glenure to a duel with pistols, but the landlord admitted that, by this time, James had seemed 'a little concerned with drink'.

MacLaren, having told much the same story, added that James had complained to Murray of 'Glenure's using him so; for that they were cousins,'[3] a claim of relationship which, however distant, certainly made his grievance more real. James seemed like a man obsessed and swore to the merchant that 'if he failed in his suspension [of the evictions] in Edinburgh, he would carry it to the British parliament; and if he failed there . . . He paused, but then went on with emphasis, that he behoved to take the only other remedy that remained.'

Seen in retrospect, these allegations, even if true, were nothing but the ravings of a drunken man. James was no longer young. He had ridden a long way, and the ale and whisky at the various taverns had certainly loosened his tongue.

However, his mission was ill-timed for, on reaching Edinburgh on 8 April, he found to his dismay that the Barons had just ended a session of their Court. The next one would not take place for three weeks, by which time the evictions on Ardsheal would have been carried out.

Indeed, on 13 April, 1752, six of the small tenants on Ardsheal estate received orders to quit their farms in just two months and two days.[4]

James must have known this for, in despair, he hurried off to find Baron Kennedy of Dunure, one of the members of the Baron's Court. The Baron listened and sympathised with the plight of the tenants, and James wrote in triumph to Charles

[3] From the evidence of Colin MacLaren, Ibid, pp. 160–2.

[4] From the Transactions of the Gaelic Society of Inverness, 'The Appin Murder', vol. XXXV, p. 346.

Stewart, his legal adviser in Maryburgh, that Baron Kennedy had been:

very kind and seem'd to sympathise much with the tenant's case. [The Baron] gave it as his private opinion [that] they should sitt their possessions for this year and that all justice would be done them and [he] thought they should take a protest against the factor's proceedings in a body. I mean the Mamore and Appin tenants. The same advise I had from all I advised with, who were not a few, and all were of the same mind [that] the tenants had a good chance once their case came before the Barons.

The arrest and imprisonment of James Mor MacGregor (or 'Drummond' as he now called himself in deference to the Duke of Perth), had been the talk of the Highlands for some months.

Originally held in Fort William, this eldest son of the now dead Rob Roy had been conveyed under close guard to Edinburgh in the previous December, where, held in the infamous Tolbooth, he was waiting to stand trial. The crime of which he stood accused was that he had been the instigator, and his brother the perpetrator, of the abduction of a young woman. Once again it seemed that James Mor was manipulating and further corrupting his younger brother.

Following his escape to the Continent after the murder of John MacLaren, Robin Oig MacGregor had enlisted in the British army and fought under Major-General Campbell of

Mamore at the Battle of Fontenoy. Wounded and taken prisoner, he was subsequently exchanged. Returning to Scotland, he reputedly joined his old regiment the Black Watch and fought at the Battle of Culloden against his own clan.[5] Discharged two years later, he married the daughter of Graham of Drunkie, an estate near Aberfoyle, but she died within a short time. Now a widower himself, he had agreed to a plan of his brother's to abduct a young widow called Jean Wright (née Key) from a farm near Balfron in Stirlingshire. The girl, whose husband had died but two months previously, was an heiress and Robin Oig was without means. A minister had been forced to marry them under the threat of cold steel. The girl had subsequently escaped but shortly afterwards had died.

James Mor had been captured, but Robin Oig, still wanted for the MacLaren murder, was now declared an outlaw and a price was put upon his head.

Allegations that James of the Glen somehow managed to get into the Edinburgh Tolbooth to visit James Mor are unproven. Had he done so he would have been saddened to see the state of degradation to which the handsome young man of the 1715 campaign had been reduced. His health ruined by imprisonment in the foul conditions of the Tolbooth, he was consumed with worry that his pregnant wife and thirteen children would be left to starve. Obviously, this was a man who was ready to leap at any chance to gain money. It was this desperation which would later lead some people to link him to another sinister crime: the murder of Colin of Glenure.

The story put about by his enemies was that James of the Glen had made a deal with James Mor whereby Robin Oig, given a gun and the means to leave the country, would shoot

[5] Dr A. H. Millar, *Gregarach*, p. 128.

Glenure. It was a persuasive theory, but it was one which James of the Glen, in his speech at the foot of the scaffold, emphatically denied.

But if James of the Glen did not visit James Mor in prison, could it have been Allan Breck who did so with the purpose of arranging that Robin Oig should shoot Glenure?

Significantly, it is known that while he was in Edinburgh James paid a bill for Allan who, after landing from France in February, had taken lodgings with a man named Hugh Stewart in a house near the Fountainswell, off the city's Royal Mile. According to one contemporary, Allan was sent over from France (it is not said by whom) with the specific object of murdering Glenure. His movements in Edinburgh are unaccountable, therefore his activities are questionable in view of later events.

It seems perfectly reasonable to believe that it was the time involved in procuring the suspension of the evictions which accounts for the length of James's stay in Edinburgh. In addition to this he may well have visited the *muileartach*, the Leith miller who was the main wholesaler for the store in Glen Duror, of which James had been left in charge.

James finally left the city on 19 April and took a week to get home. He spread the good news that the evictions in Ardsheal had been suspended. His mind was at last at rest. He had done everything within his power to save six poor Gaelic-speaking country men with little knowledge of the law.

CHAPTER 7

Pursuit Unseen

When Colin Campbell of Glenure was told of James's success, he realised that it presented a serious challenge to his authority as factor. His job was on the line. Whatever his own personal feelings – he is said to have sympathised with the tenants at one time – he had to prove his loyalty and do something to quash the rumours that he was playing a double game. In addition, he could not afford to lose his position as factor: the building of Glenure House had proved expensive and, married as he was to the daughter of a leading Whig family, he had little choice but to support the Hanoverian cause. He had to make a decisive move. So it was that, on the first day of May, he too set out for Edinburgh. Five days later, on the fifth, Glenure contrived to get the Bill of Suspension over-ruled by Lord Haining.[1]

He then rode home immediately. The days were getting longer and he made good time. In the last stage of the journey he most likely left the military road at the head of Loch Etive and took a short cut across the hill to Glenure. Following the steep track down the river, he reached his own house on the

[1] Lord Haining was a judge who did not earn fame or respect by his attainments. The outspoken Mr Ramsay says of him that he was a man 'who, with a slight knowledge of the law, had been made a judge by the interest of potent friends'. *Ochterarder Papers*, p. 323.

flat ground at the foot of the glen on Saturday, 9 May.

He must have rejoiced to be home with his wife and his two little girls. Argyll in May is a magical place, when the barren land of winter comes suddenly alive. His herd of fine cattle, of which he was so proud, grazed on the meadows round the house. Soon, within a week or two, they would be driven to higher ground.

Colin, after his long ride to and from Edinburgh, must have wanted nothing more than to stay at Glenure, but obedient to orders he had received in the city, he had only a brief weekend at home. Absorbed in his family and the business of his estate, he appears to have been unaware that his every movement was being watched.

On 30 April, the day before Colin set out for Edinburgh, Allan Breck, who had been visiting friends in Rannoch, had reappeared at Acharn. Shortly afterwards, he had gone to stay with James Stewart (young Fasnacloich), at his home in Glen Creran, just a mile down the glen from Glenure. As a soldier trained in reconnaissance, Allan would have had little difficulty in keeping Colin Campbell under surveillance.

On Monday, 11 May, Colin set out for Maryburgh (now known as Fort William) with the purpose of evicting some of the tenants on Lochiel's forfeited estate. With him went his nephew Mungo, illegitimate son of his brother Barcaldine, who had just recently qualified as a lawyer, and his servant, a young man called John MacKenzie.

The three of them rode from Glenure House across the river Creran and then up the old hill track into *Gleann an Fhiodh* that leads to Loch Leven. At the ferry they were joined by Donald Kennedy, a sheriff's officer from Inveraray, who was coming to oversee the evictions about to be carried out.

The big, flat-bottomed craft, with strong men pulling on the sweeps,[2] carried the travellers and their horses across the narrows of the loch to the Lochaber shore. Once landed, they headed for the Cameron estates of Lochiel where, as Colin had been warned, threats to kill him had been made.

Meanwhile, back in Appin on that same Monday evening, Allan Breck and James Stewart returned to Acharn from Fasnacloich. Allan Breck borrowed some of James of the Glen's clothes with the excuse that his flashy French uniform, with its feathered hat, made him conspicuous in the countryside. James afterwards claimed that he did not know how Allan had got into them, his foster-son being a large fellow and himself a small man. The garments in question were a pair of blue-and-white striped trousers, probably of homespun weave, and a short, black coat with white metal or 'silver' buttons. (Allan, James's eldest son, had a coat very much the same.) Little did anyone guess how notorious these articles of clothing would soon become.

Allan found James in one of the fields near his house with his men. They had been planting potatoes on ridges with deep furrows on either side. It was back-breaking work and they were sitting down having a rest. Allan joined them and they all conversed in Gaelic about the people in Glen Creran, or so John Mor MacColl later remembered. Allan gave them a hand for a while. Then he and James walked back the short distance to Acharn – the only time, as was vouched for, that the two men were entirely alone. This cannot have been for more than ten minutes as, on entering the house, James was given a message that his friend, Campbell of Airds, from whom he was renting another farm, wanted to see him. He left immediately and it was nearly nightfall before he returned home.

[2] 'Sweeps' are long oars with broad blades.

James and his wife Margaret, renowned for their hospitality, asked Allan to join the family for a late supper. The house was so small, however, that he and Charles, James's younger son, had to spend the night sleeping on straw in the barn. The barn may have been attached to the far-end of the house, partly partitioned from the living quarters, or in a building nearby.

What did they discuss in the darkness of that early summer night? They had just heard the news that Campbell of Glenure had over-ruled the suspension of the tenant's evictions and no doubt they ranted on about how James had been betrayed. Charles was very impressionable and Allan, the swashbuckling soldier of fortune, must have been a hero to the boy.

On the morning of the next day, Tuesday, 12 May, James went off to meet his chief, Stewart of Appin, before Allan had even risen. When eventually he did get up, he went off to Ballachulish House where (as would seem to have been previously arranged) he was joined by young Fasnacloich.

From Ballachulish the two of them went first to Carnoch in Glencoe, the home of MacDonald of Glencoe, whose stepmother, Isabel, was a sister of Charles Stewart of Ardsheal. Having stayed there for about an hour they went their separate ways. Allan Breck crossed the Ballachulish Ferry to the house of Cameron of Callart, whose wife was another sister of Ardsheal, on the Lochaber shore.

From there he is believed to have pursued Colin Campbell and his companions, constantly watching their movements without, so he thought, being seen. Colin or one of his party, however, must have caught a glimpse of him and guessed what he was about, for Mungo Campbell, Colin's nephew, writing from Fort William on 23 May, told of how 'Allan Breck Stewart, who had made threats against Glenure, and had come from the Highlands to the Low Scott country . . . kept pace with Glenure and me back again all the way to Lochaber.'[3]

Allan Breck spent the night of Tuesday, 12 May, in the house of Cameron of Callart. What was arranged there can only be imagined. Local legend tells of a party of Camerons rowing across Loch Leven at night to lie in wait in the wood of Lettermore. These and other stories certainly indicate that a conspiracy to kill Glenure, by one means or another, was planned.

It is known that on the following day, Wednesday, Allan Breck returned to Ballachulish House where he remained for the night. Young Ballachulish, the laird's son, was absent; he was, in fact, at Acharn,[4] a fact of some significance in view of forthcoming events.

By now it was Wednesday evening. The evictions at Ardsheal were due to take place on Friday. There were only two days to go.

[3] *Trial of James Stewart*, edited by D. N. Mackay, p. 305.

[4] *The Appin Murder* by General McArthur, p. 98.

CHAPTER 8

Death on the Road through Lettermore

C olin Campbell of Glenure had reached Lochiel's estates on the Monday evening; the same day he had left home. On his instructions, several farmers in Mamore and Callart were turned out. Some, however, were allowed to remain for a year on condition that they went to Maryburgh immediately and took the oath of allegiance to the King.

James of the Glen is known to have stated publicly that, whatever happened, he would abide by the law. He was advised (it is not known by whom) that the tenants might still be saved if a formal protest against the evictions was made *in situ* before a lawyer and witnesses of good repute. In near desperation, he tried to get this arranged. Time was now very short. There was only a day to go before Glenure was due to arrive in Ardsheal.

At eight o'clock on the morning of Thursday, 14 May, James sent his servant, John Beg MacColl, to Maryburgh with a letter to Charles Stewart, a lawyer (called a 'writer' in Scots) telling him to come with all speed to Appin. 'You must be here without fail this night [that of the 14th], if [necessary] you should hyre a horse, as everything must go without a person can act, and that I can trust.'[1]

John Beg, a young man of twenty-seven and very fast on his feet, dashed off to Kentallen. There he found John Mor MacColl and the inn-keeper, John Breck Maccombie (who had hosted the fateful meeting of the Campbells and the Stewarts on New Year's Eve). Maccombie was busy preparing for the arrival of Colin Campbell of Glenure and his party that same night. Nonetheless, realising the urgency of John Beg's mission, he seems to have been one of the crew of the boat which took him across the mouth of Loch Leven to Onich – a quicker way to get to Maryburgh than by crossing the Ballachulish Ferry.

Approaching the town at 'the end of the three-mile water', MacColl actually met Colin Campbell riding with his servant, John MacKenzie, a stout lad of nineteen, very close to his side. Forty-eight-year-old Donald Kennedy, the writer from Inveraray who had been summoned to carry out the evictions, was following on foot.

Reaching Maryburgh by mid-day, MacColl found to his dismay that Charles Stewart, the writer whom he had been sent so urgently to fetch, was away from home. William Stewart, the merchant (James's first cousin and brother-in-law), told him that Charles had gone to the Braes of Lochaber and would not be back until the evening. John Beg asked if he should wait, but William Stewart thought it unnecessary: Charles, no runner, could get to Appin quicker by boat, and the merchant promised to pass on the message to the writer himself. John Beg was apparently now so flustered that he forgot James's other request, which was to ask William for the money for the four cows that James had bought for him. He

[1] From *Notable Scottish Trials*, edited by D. N. Mackay,

was in too much of a hurry even to accept the 'victuals' which William Stewart offered. He just had time to gulp down a dram before rushing off once more. Tearing back with his news, John Beg actually overtook Glenure and his party, who were on what was called the 'horse road' by the sea, he having taken a quicker way on a higher path.

Approaching the ferry, he found the ferryman cutting seaweed. The ferryman, knowing the Crown factor was coming (some accounts say that he was already there) and that he would have to make two trips, asked John Beg to wait and cross with the horses. But the young man argued that the tide was running too strongly for it to be safe to carry the animals and persuaded the ferryman to make a special journey to the Appin shore. Landing, he met the ferryman on the Appin side, who told him that he 'was going to meet Glenure [which he subsequently did] and that the new tenants, that were come to Ardsheal, had come to Glen Duror with their cattle and were to take possession the next day.'

John Beg replied that he, personally, 'did not believe' the new tenants 'would get possession till their warrands were seen'.

Beg ran on but had not gone far before he met Alexander Stewart, 'old Ballachulish', who was obviously hanging about waiting to waylay Glenure. John Beg told him of his fruitless errand and of the ferryman's report that the new tenants were ready to move in. Alexander instructed him 'to tell his master, if he would send for him, he would go along with him to see Glenure's warrand'.[2]

Promising this, John Beg went on along the road through the wood of Lettermore. Little did he know, as he trotted along a steep part of the track below a birch tree, that a man was

[2] *Notable Scottish Trials*, edited by D. N. Mackay, p. 169–75. This and other statements were taken from the evidence of John Beg MacColl.

resting his gun on a branch, his sights fixed upon the road.

Meeting a local farmer, John Roy Livingstone, Beg told him of his failed mission and of his haste to get home. Exhausted, he did stop briefly at the inn at Kentallen, where he called for half a 'mutchkin of aquavitae', but was in such a hurry that he did not even sit down. However, he did tell the inn-keeper, John Breck Maccombie, of his futile journey to Maryburgh before dashing on. No doubt the inn was in tumult as they made last-minute preparations before the arrival of Glenure and his party.

John Beg MacColl was probably the man whom a local woman called Mor MacIntyre saw running very fast through the wood a short while later. Otherwise it could have been Grey Ewan MacKenzie, a public messenger from Maryburgh, who carried a letter from William Stewart to his brother-in-law, James, advising him to tell the tenants to refuse Glenure's order to move. 'As there will be no troops, they ought to repel force by force, and take their hazard of the consequences; as it can be no more than violent profits, which is often modified in inferior courts.' 'Violent profits', in the case of illegal occupation, gave the landowner the right to charge the highest rent that he could find.

John Beg and Grey Ewan reached Acharn to find that James of the Glen, who had been working with his men sowing barley, had just come into the house with mud up to his knees. Obviously here, as elsewhere in Appin, the cows had been driven up to the *airidhs* in the hills so that their dung could be cleared from the barns and carted out to fertilise the crops.

Earlier that day Allan Breck, a guest at Ballachulish House, in his borrowed country clothes, had actually helped them for a short time. But hard work, particularly this task, was not to his liking and, at about mid-morning, he wandered back to Ballachulish House saying he was going to fish the burn. Afterwards, it was remembered that he borrowed a rod and line but could not find a hook. Resourceful, however, when necessary, he contrived to make one, presumably out of a pin.

Gleann a Chaolais, the burn that runs past Ballachulish House, plunges down a steep glen. From the hillside above it, Allan had a clear view across the narrows of Loch Leven where the big, flat-bottomed ferry plied back and forth.

Archibald Macinnes, the one-eyed ferryman (or '*Portair Cam*') who, ironically, was supposed to have second sight, was sitting talking in Gaelic to another man on the Appin side when he heard a 'host', or a cough behind his back. Turning, he saw Allan Breck who asked him if Glenure had crossed the ferry from Lochaber to Appin. Macinnes assured him he had not and Allan Breck wandered off towards the high road. He was wearing, so the ferryman remembered, 'a dun-coloured big coat and did not have a fishing rod in his hand'.[3]

Colin Campbell and his companions, their business completed, were by now riding from Maryburgh. It was a beautiful, early May day and the Argyll countryside was at its most glorious. But Colin and his companions hardly felt the sunshine nor heard the curlew's call. They spoke little. Twisting in their saddles, they scanned the hillside above them, glancing backwards to see if they were being followed. Colin had been forewarned of danger. There were many in Lochaber who called him a traitor to his Cameron mother's name. Death threats had been made against him and John MacKenzie, his servant, rode with him knee to knee, effectively shielding him with his body and preventing a marksman from getting a clear shot from above.

[3] From the evidence of Archibald Macinnes; *Notable Scottish Trials*, p. 147.]

There were men waiting in hiding, so the legend goes, but with Mackenzie blocking their target none dared to shoot. Colin is known to have been thankful when the narrows of Loch Leven came in sight for, once across in Appin, he believed he would be safe.

Reaching the ferry at *Caolas Mhic Pharuig*, on the Lochaber shore, Colin sent John MacKenzie over first with the horses. While he waited, he talked to some local people about the way it was run. He suggested that, as in other places, a ferryman should be employed, who could be given some farmland for

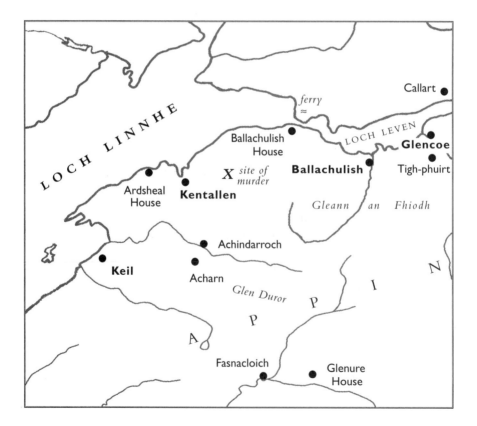

thirty Scots pounds a year in rent. The tenants, who under the existing arrangement maintained the ferry and received the fares themselves, were indignant. This was just another instance of interference by the factor, who in their eyes had no business to deny their established rights.

According to the Dewar Manuscripts, one-eyed Archibald Macinnes was the ferryman at the *Caolas Mhic Pharuig* side. All other accounts, however, claim that he was on the Appin side when Colin landed and he waylaid him to warn of impending danger. Speaking in Gaelic, he beseeched him not to take the road to the south through the wood of Lettermore but to go home through *Gleann an Fhiodh* (Glen of the Wood) or else to go to Kentallen by boat. Colin, however, did not listen. He had left his mother's country behind him, he said, and he knew he was safe in Appin.

The double ferry journey had taken so long that it was now late afternoon. John Mackenzie was waiting with the horses and they set off along the old road which ran at first by the shore. They were heading for Kentallen where they planned to stay the night. The day was becoming warmer and Donald Kennedy, the sheriff's officer, who was walking, asked MacKenzie to carry his heavy coat. MacKenzie put it across the front of his saddle but, on reaching a place where the incoming tide had undermined the road, he dismounted to lead his horse and the coat slipped off the pommel on to the ground.

The road left the shore and Alexander Stewart, 'old Ballachulish', joined them on foot. Colin dismounted in politeness to the senior man and the two walked together for some way. Neither of them saw Allan Breck, but Allan most certainly saw them.

Glenure and Ballachulish, talking in a friendly manner and avoiding the subject of the evictions, suddenly noticed a great-coat lying in the mud. Colin called out to those in front and asked to whom it belonged. MacKenzie shouted back that it was the sheriff officer's, which he had dropped. He hurried back to collect it and then followed behind.

No one has ever questioned the innocence of this young man; he seems to have been devoted to his master, whom he had guarded with his own life. Yet the incident of the dropped coat inevitably raises the question as to whether it was mere coincidence or a signal that Glenure now rode without protection.

And what part did 'old Ballachulish' have in the affair? He had not been 'out' in the '45, being too advanced in years to take the field, and for this reason had been spared the forfeiture of his land. His eldest son, however, who had risen for the Prince, had been killed; and four of his nephews had been wounded. So he had plenty of reason to hate the Hanoverian regime. Bearing this in mind, one wonders whether he was waiting to meet Colin simply out of courtesy to a neighbour, or was purposely waylaying him for some more sinister reason?

Approaching Ballachulish House, the old man is said to have tried to persuade Colin and his companions to stay the night. This must have simply been a gesture of Highland hospitality as he almost certainly knew that rooms in the inn at Kentallen had been reserved. Colin predictably refused, explaining that his cousin, Campbell of Ballieveolan, was coming to meet him at Kentallen and was probably waiting there by now.

Parting with Ballachulish, he began the ascent of the hill with Kennedy now leading the way on foot. Colin and his nephew, Mungo Campbell, rode together where the width of the track allowed two horses abreast. Shortly, however, it narrowed on to a precipitous slope where the hill rose almost vertically above.

Colin reigned in, telling Mungo to go ahead. The younger man pushed past and almost as he did so a shot rang out behind. Instantly, the terrified horses plunged forward. Some say Colin's leg was crushed against a gatepost. He cried out, 'Oh, I am dead! He's going to shoot you! Save yourself!'

The old road through Lettermore (which is now difficult to trace)

Mungo jumped off his horse in a split second and rushed back. He was horrified by what he found. Then he sprinted a few yards up the hill in the direction from which the shot had come. He saw a man with a gun in his hand scrambling upwards. He wore, Mungo afterwards testified, a dun-coloured coat and breeches.

Fit as he was, there was no way Mungo could catch the assailant, and he rushed back to his uncle and helped him gently from his horse. Colin clutched at him in agony, fumbling with his waistcoat, trying to find the wound.

Mungo saw it soon enough. Blood from a ruptured liver was pouring to the ground. Later, it was found that Colin had been hit by two bullets, fired from a long-barrelled gun. This type of weapon, then popular in the Highlands for deer stalking, was loaded with two lead shots. The first, which fitted the bore, was the most accurate. The second, called the 'chaser', had a longer range. Colin Campbell, fired on from behind, had received the full impact of both, one on either side of his spine.

The sheriff's officer, walking ahead along the track, swung round as he heard the shot and Mungo's cry, 'The villain has killed my dear uncle!' Mungo managed to tell the sheriff that he had seen only one man. Kennedy afterwards admitted that he had been too terrified to ask any more questions at that moment.

John Mackenzie, riding up the slope behind, also heard the shot which he thought came from a firelock but, as he admitted afterwards, he was very confused.

At the time, he arrived breathless at the scene. He had only a moment to look at his master, lying bleeding to death on the ground, before Mungo thrust the reins of the best of the horses into his hands and told him to ride for his life to the inn at Kentallen and bring help. Mackenzie did as he was ordered, nearly killing the animal he rode. Meanwhile, Mungo Campbell and the sheriff's officer, the latter shaking with terror, were left to watch Colin gasping in agony as his blood soaked into the ground.

Colin Campbell of Glenure, a young man in the prime of life, died within an hour of being shot, on that May evening, in the wood of Lettermore.

CHAPTER 9

No Name upon the Stone

The young John Mackenzie arrived at Kentallen inn, both he and his horse exhausted, but there was no one there who could help him. In desperation, he forced his spent mount on to Acharn.

As the light faded, James of the Glen was just coming in from the fields. He was inside talking to Robert Stewart, of the old mill at Duror, and Robert's son when they heard the pounding of hooves and then a thunderous hammering on the door. On opening it and seeing the poor, sweating beast, its sides heaving, James said, *'Co sam bith am marcaiche, cha leis fhein an t'each.'* (Whoever that rider may be, the horse is not his own.)

Then he recognized John Mackenzie and when he learned what had happened, James turned to the miller and said, *'Ah, Rob, co sam bith an ciontach, 's mise an crionlach.'* (Ah, Rob, whoever is the culprit, I shall be the victim.)[1] Apparently, during the discussion James had asked if Colin had been shot, which some have taken as an indication that he had guessed such a thing might occur. He wrung his hands in desperate

[1] Ibid, Appendix XVII, p. 367.

The dark panelled room
in Glenure House where
Colin Campbell was laid
out after his brutal murder
(photograph by Roy Summers)

Ruins of Acharn, James of the Glen's home. It can be
reached by taking a side road, marked to Inshaig, which branches
off the A828 almost oppposite Duror Inn *(photograph by Malcolm MacGregor)*

The path leading up to the ruined Keil Chapel wherein lies the grave of James of the Glen

Caolasnacoan, the heugh of Corrynakeigh (the high ground where Allan Breck lay in hiding) lies above the fir trees *(photograph by Malcolm MacGregor)*

sorrow and prayed that innocent people would not be brought into trouble.

Immediately, he changed his muddy clothes for clean ones and set off with his two sons to offer what help he could to Colin Campbell, hoping that he was still alive. But even as they were mounting their horses, James's wife rushed from the house to call them back. The Campbells would be gathering round the injured man, she warned them. They might be attacked and even killed. James must have realized she was right. Sending some of his servants and neighbours to the scene instead, he instructed Mackenzie on the quickest way to Glen Duror, telling him that Ballieveolan might be there. Probably, James guessed he would be needed to defend his home now that his situation had become even more tenuous.

This was the story told afterwards by James's sons, but the fact that he did not go to help Colin Campbell counted against him at the murder trial.

Meanwhile, as darkness deepened, Mungo Campbell grew more desperate as he waited by his dead uncle's side. Finally, guessing that MacKenzie had failed to find anyone at Kentallen, he sent the sheriff's officer back to Alexander Stewart of Ballachulish, begging him to bring help. In a short time, the old laird and his nephew Donald, together with numerous locals, all chattering in Gaelic, appeared. Mungo later claimed that most of them seemed to relish the sight of the factor lying dead in his own blood. Nonetheless, it was Donald Stewart who helped carry the body to the shore, stumbling in near darkness along the just visible track.

Next day, the very Friday when the evictions he had arranged were due to be carried out, the corpse of Colin of Glenure was taken by boat to Larach. From there it was carried down the old track, which runs through *Gleann an Fhiodh*, along which he had ridden only four days before. Reaching Glenure House, he was laid out in a first-floor bedroom, panelled with dark pine. The two surgeons who examined his body were Alexander Campbell and Patrick Campbell of Achnaba. The latter stated that the two wounds were two and a half inches apart, which indicated that they had been inflicted by the same gun at short range.

The shock to Janet, Colin's young widow, who had seen him ride away so full of life on the Monday morning, must have been very great. Nonetheless, she acted with great courage and determination, as was remarked upon at the time. She decided to delay the funeral so that her father could attend (he was actually prevented by illness from doing so); then the coffin was taken to Ardchattan, the twelfth-century Priory on

The middle slab (cracked) is believed to be that of Colin Campbell of Glenure, murdered on 14 May, 1752. It lies within the family burial ground of the Campbells of Barcaldine within the twelfth-century Ardchattan Priory on the north shore of Loch Etive in Argyll.

the north-east shore of Loch Etive. The most probable route would appear to have been down Glen Creran, along the south shore of Loch Creran and then over the hill and down *Gleann Salach*, which converges upon Loch Etive about a mile to the east of Ardchattan.

Colin's grave, in the family burial ground of the Campbells of Barcaldine, was covered by an unmarked slab. The fact that his family were only too aware of the danger that it might be vandalised by local Jacobites were his name inscribed, is significant of the fear and mistrust which existed, even amongst neighbours, following the political upheaval of the Rising of 1745.

Nothing remains in Ardchattan churchyard save for a now cracked stone. Yet Colin Campbell of Glenure is immortalised in a Gaelic song written by his foster-brother, the poet Duncan Ban MacIntyre, who poured out his heart both in sorrow and anger against his murderer.

Tha mo ghruaidhean aie seacadh,
Gun dion uair air mo rasgaibh,
Mu 'n sgeul a chualas o'n Apainn
A ghluais a' chaismeachd ud dùinn:
Fear Ghlinn Iubhair a dhith oirnn.

My cheeks are grown wizened,
mine eyes not dry for a moment,
because of the news from Appin,
which roused us in such alarm:
we are bereaved of Glenure.

B'sin an corp àlainn
N' uair bha thu roimhe seo'd shlàinte,

That was the beautiful body,
when thou was in thine pristine vigour

B'e do choimeas an drèagan
No 'n t-seabhag 'sna speuran;
Co bu choslach r' a chèile
Ach iad fèin agus tu?

Thy counterpart was the dragon,
or the hawk in the heavens;
who did resemble each other,
if not thou and these?

'S e do chadal gu siorraidh
A dh' fhàg m'aigneadh cho tiamhaidh,
'S tric smaointeana diomhain
A' tighinn gu dian orm as ùr;
'S trom a dh' fhàs orm an iargain,
'S goirte t'àr -sa na 'm fiabhras,
Mo chomhalt'àlainn deas ciatach
An déis a riabadh gu dlùth.
Mile mollachd do 'n laimh sin
A ghabh cothrom is fàth ort,
A thug an comas do 'n làmhach
'N uair chuir e 'n Spàin teach r'a shùil.
Sgeula soilleir a b' àill leam,
Gun cluinnt' am follais aif càch
E bhith dol ri cromaig le fàradh,
Gus am miosa dhà-san na dhùinn.

'Tis thy sleep enduring for ever,

hath left my spirit so mournful;

often do futile reflections

rush upon me anew;

anguish hath grown heavy upon me,

thy death is more painful than fever —

my splendid, keen, fine foster-brother,

hath been utterly rent.

A thousand curses on him

who seized his chance and surprised thee,

whose hand released the gun-shot,

when he brought the Spanish gun to the aim,

It would be bright news which would please me,

were it openly heard by all,

that he went to the gallows by a ladder,

till his plight was worse than ours.

Then finally with great sadness.

'S e dh' fhàg mise for èislean

Bhith 'n diugh ag innseadh do bheusan

'S nach rig thu dh' èisdeachd mo sgiùil.

'Tis this hath left me afflicted,

that today I am telling thy virtues,

and thou wilt not come to hear my tale.[2]

---

[2] Extracts from the lament of Duncan Ban MacIntyre.

CHAPTER 10

The Nights of Fear

As darkness fell on the evening of the murder, Allan Breck was found hiding in a goat-house on the moor of Ballachulish by Katherine Macinnes, a young girl of twenty-two. Katherine was one of old Ballachulish's servants and had probably come to milk the goats. Seeing the lights of torches below them from the hill, Allan asked her, 'what was the occasion of the stir in the town?' She told him Glenure had been murdered. 'Who was his killer?' he then wanted to know, but she could not tell him. He then asked her to take a message to Donald Stewart (nephew of Ballachulish), which he would then take to James of the Glen. Allan Breck wanted his foster-father to send him money. The girl found Donald just returned from carrying Glenure's corpse to the boat.

Donald later admitted that he had then climbed up the hill to the goat-house where he discovered Allan Breck. Despite the fact that it was dark, he claimed that Allan was still wearing a great coat over a short, dark coat with metal buttons. He vowed that, having charged him with the murder, Allan had denied any involvement. As a deserter from the Hanoverian army, Allan knew he was an obvious suspect and so 'it was necessary for him to leave the kingdom'. He desperately needed money and begged Donald Stewart to ask James for it on his behalf. He must also tell him that he would be hiding in the wilds of Caolasnacoan.[1]

Afterwards, perhaps by moonlight, Allan somehow made his way to Glencoe. John MacDonald was asleep when, at three or four in the morning, he heard a loud rapping on the window and found Allan at the door. He told him of Glenure's murder and that he had come to say goodbye – he was going 'to leave the country and take the moor road leading to Rannoch'. His stepmother, Isabel (sister of the exiled Charles Stewart of Ardsheal), had by this time appeared and, eager to know the details of what had happened, asked Allan to come in. Refusing, Allan Breck vanished as suddenly as he had come.

Thursday night must have been sleepless one for James and his family at Acharn. Early next morning Donald Stewart appeared with the message from Allan Breck. James's reaction was typical of the generosity of the man. He certainly had his faults, fondness for the bottle being one, but his goodness of heart and concern for others is nowhere better shown.

Allan's demand had placed him in a quandary for he had no ready cash. He had spent everything on the journey to Edinburgh and on legal advice for the Ardsheal tenants. But he was a cattle dealer and so he had debtors. The merchant William Stewart, his first cousin and brother-in-law, for example, still owed him the money for four milk cows. And he

[1] From the evidence of Donald Stewart; *Notable Scottish Trials*, pp. 147–9.

had also purchased a horse for Cameron of Glen Nevis who had not paid him either.

James did not hesitate in complying with Allan's request. He summoned Alexander Stewart, a first cousin of Allan Breck (their fathers were brothers), who lived nearby. Alexander was one of the 'packmen', who carried messages and sold household necessities, such as pots and pans, in Highland villages at that time. James told him to go to William Stewart in Maryburgh and ask for eight pounds for the cows, telling him that they would not be delivered until paid for. Then he was to go to Glen Nevis and get the money for the horse.

The packman must have left at once and later that morning John Stewart, young Ballachulish, arrived at Acharn to find the house in a state of confusion. James and Margaret decided that their youngest boy, Charles, and their daughter, Elizabeth, who had gone on a visit to Fasnacloich House, must be summoned home immediately.

The possession of weapons in the Highlands, illegal since the Rising of 1715, had again been forbidden in 1746. However, most families had muskets and swords of some description hidden below the thatch. The Stewarts knew that at any moment Red Coats from Fort William would appear to search for the murder weapon. They would tear the house apart.

One long-barrelled deer gun was propped up, still loaded with shot, in the brew-house, which was normally kept locked. The other, hidden under the 'girnel' or meal-chest in the barn, was unloaded and had been left uncleaned.

They had to be hidden at once. Dugald and John Beg MacColl were told to conceal them on the hill.

At the same time, Margaret Stewart told her sixteen-year-old servant-girl, Katherine MacColl, to take a sack containing Allan Breck's French uniform and hide it well away from the house. The girl (who could not write) afterwards testified that 'as she was going up the brae . . . [she] was overtaken by Dugald and John Beg MacColl, who had some guns and swords.' [2] Dugald MacColl hid the clothes for her on the moor. The next night, however, Mrs Stewart asked her to collect the hidden clothes and put them at the back of the brew-house. Her mistress then swore the girl to secrecy; a trust which, under pressure, she was to betray.

In the meantime, the packman had reached Maryburgh. He found William Stewart, but the merchant insisted that he had no cash available as he had paid out large sums that morning. William told the packman to go on to Glen Nevis to collect the money for the 'stoned' (perhaps lame) horse and to come back to the town the next day. This time the packman met the merchant's wife in the street. She gave him three guineas for two of the cows, which were sent from Acharn forthwith.

The packman returned to Acharn to find James away from home. Shortly, a message arrived saying that he and his eldest son, Allan, had been taken prisoner at the nearby house of Inshaig and were held under close arrest. The packman and Margaret walked the short distance to Inshaig where they found her husband and son guarded by a company of English soldiers. They were allowed to talk to James in Gaelic, which fortunately the soldiers did not understand. The packman produced the three guineas (evidently, he never received the money for the horse), and James took another two from a green purse and handed them to his wife. She passed them over to the packman.

James and his son were then taken to Fort William, being

[2] From the evidence of Katherine MacColl; Ibid, pp. 143–4.]

forced to walk through the night.

Margaret Stewart, still keeping her wits about her, returned to Acharn where, later that evening, she gave Allan Breck's French uniform to the packman and told him to take it, together with the five guineas, to Caolasnacoan, where, if he did not find Allan, he was to give both money and clothes to the bouman, John Breck MacColl. Before he set off, she gave him some supper. Then, when it was dark, she sent him on his way with clear instructions: he was not to go to John Breck MacColl's house, 'lest anybody might see them'.

The packman understandably took fright, saying he did not want to go such a long way on his own at night. Indeed, it was some distance, as Caolasnacoan (the Narrows of the Dog) is on the south side of Loch Leven, at least ten miles from Acharn. The indomitable Mrs Stewart, however, insisted that he go. Both her other servants had been arrested and taken to Fort William and there was no one else she could send. She told him to take his sister Margaret with him, which he did, and the two went together as far as Larach in Glencoe, where they parted in the light of the May dawn.

The packman then went on alone to Caolasnacoan, in those days considered 'a desert' on the south shore of Loch Leven. He left the clothes, as instructed, at the foot of a fir tree some distance from the bouman's house, but when he went up to the low, thatched cottage, he met MacColl himself.

Forty-year-old John Breck MacColl was another of the impoverished tenants sheltered by James of the Glen. Thanks to James's influence with his chief, Stewart of Appin, he had been given this stretch of hill in 'steel-bow' – a form of letting by which the landlord supplied the stock and shared the profits until, when the lease expired, any beasts which survived were returned. Likewise, MacColl had cotters working part time for him in return for being allowed to keep a few animals of their own. By May, the corn had been planted on the cultivated land and the women had driven the cattle to the *airidhs*, or grazings on high ground.

When it came time for the bouman to give evidence, he stated that 'upon the evening of the said Saturday [16 May], Katherine MacColl, spouse to Hugh MacColl in Kaolisnacoan [sic], told him that she had seen a man in the heugh of Corrynakeigh that day . . . and was greatly frighted.' He had advised her that though 'there used to be bogles seen in that place . . . she must take no notice of what she had seen, for fear of frightening the women of the town, and prevent them from attending their cattle in that part.' But he admitted that his real reason for telling her this 'was for fear it would be known that it was Allan Breck she saw'.

However, at the time, MacColl insisted that he had not seen Allan Breck, and it was only when the packman explained his mission that MacColl admitted that Breck was in the heugh of Corrynakeigh (where the cattle were grazing) above his house. Alexander could go up the hill and whistle, and Allan Breck would come to him.

But the packman, after two sleepless nights, had had enough. He pointed out the fir tree where he had left the clothes and gave the five guineas to MacColl to pass on to Allan Breck. He then went to MacColl's small farmhouse and slept. Later, the two had a meal together before the packman set off home.

Arriving at Acharn on the Sunday evening (17 May), he was asked by an anxious Margaret Stewart if he had seen Allan Breck. He told her that he had not actually set eyes on him but that he had given both the clothes and the money to the bouman. She seemed satisfied with this, as he later explained during the trial.[3]

For his part, the bouman told the court how he had met Allan Breck on the Saturday, prior to the arrival of Alexander Stewart, the packman. He had, he said, been in 'a fir bush near Aldavoin, at the foot of the heugh of Corrynakeigh in Koalisnacoan [when] he heard a whistle; and, upon looking up, saw Allan Breck Stewart, at a little distance, beckoning him to come towards him, which he did'. He had heard the day before from two women who came up Glencoe 'that Glenure was murdered on Thursday evening in the wood of Lettermore; and that two people were seen going from the place . . . and that he, Allan, was said to be one of them.'

Defending himself, Allan Breck swore 'he had no concern in it; and that if his information was right, there was but one person about the murder.' Understandably, he feared that 'as he was idle in the country, he was sure he would be suspected of it.' MacColl, however, 'did not believe him when he said he had no hand in the assassination . . . and pressed him to leave the place, lest he should bring himself and his family into trouble'. Allan Breck admitted that 'he did not doubt but the family of Ardsheal would be suspected of the murder . . . it was probable that James of the Glen and Allan Stewart his son might be taken into custody about it.' Moreover, he was afraid that the boy's tongue 'was not so good as his father's'.

The strength of the prosecutor's case was to rest mainly upon this evidence of the bouman, who is believed to have concocted most of it on the way to James's trial in Inveraray. MacColl also claimed that Allan Breck had told him that if money did not reach him by other means that he (MacColl)

[3] From the evidence of Alexander Stewart, travelling packman in Appin; Ibid, pp. 179–82.

must go to Maryburgh with a letter to William Stewart with whom credit had been arranged.

The bouman said that he had refused to do this but, regardless, Allan searched about under the trees, found a wood pigeon's feather and made it into a quill. He then made ink out of some powder, which he had in a horn in his pocket, and wrote a letter which he ordered the bouman to take to the merchant. (William Stewart's wife, unbeknown to either of them, was probably at that very moment handing over the money for her cows to the packman.)

MacColl protested strongly. He had been told (presumably by the two women) that everyone going to Fort William was being searched. Allan Breck insisted that anyone could hide a letter but, in the event of his being caught, 'he must eat it before it was found'.

The bouman went on to say that Allan had then asked him to 'go to Callart or Glencoe's house for a peck of meal for him,' which he refused to do, whereupon Allan Breck, clearly annoyed, had gone off saying he would see him the next day. He was wearing the dun-coloured great coat, black short coat and 'blue trousers strip'd with white', which were produced as exhibits in court.

Early next morning (Sunday, 17 May), the bouman got up 'to look at his corns', which must have been just coming through the ground. He saw a man, who he first thought was Allan Breck, coming up the glen. It turned out to be Alexander Stewart, the packman.

MacColl continued to relate how, after he had gone to bed, he heard someone knocking at the window and when he went out in his shirt, he found Allan Breck. He told Breck that his uncle's son had come with five guineas and some clothes. Allan complained that 'there was but little money, but hoped it would do his business'. MacColl said that 'he was afraid he would starve among the heather', but Allan assured him that he 'had no occasion for victuals, but wanted a drink very much'. MacColl went back into his house and brought out the five guineas, along with some whey, or milk and water, in a noggin. Then he gave Breck the clothes from below the fir tree.

During their conversation, Allan Breck learned that James and his eldest son had indeed been arrested, and he responded by saying that 'it would not signify much, as there could be no proof against them.' He had repeated his fear, however, that 'Allan Stewart might be betrayed by his own tongue.' Then, having arranged with the bouman to meet him next morning, he vanished into the night.

Morning came with no sign of him. Only the borrowed clothes, the striped trousers and the coat with the metal buttons, together with the noggin which had held the whey, were left near the bouman's house. Terrified of being implicated in the murder, he hastily hid the garments within the cleft of a rock.[4]

[4] From the evidence of John Breck MacColl, bouman to Appin in Caolasnacoan; Ibid, pp. 182–6.

CHAPTER 11

Imprisonment of James of the Glen

At Fort William, James and his son were denied their legal rights; they were kept in close confinement and totally forbidden contact with anyone from outside. This was in direct contempt of the law. An Act of Parliament in 1701 had stipulated that a prisoner whose offence was not bailable, and who heard nothing about the date of his trial, was entitled to 'run his letters', that is, to apply to the Court to have his trial brought on. The judge was bound to issue, within twenty-four hours, instructions to the prosecutors compelling them to bring the case to trial within sixty days. If it did not begin by that time, the prisoner was entitled to be set at liberty. Thus, if James had been able to 'run his letters', the case would have had to be heard in Edinburgh prior to the Inveraray autumn circuit. There was no evidence that would induce an Edinburgh jury to hang any man, so James had to be deprived of an Edinburgh trial.

Colonel Crawford, in command of the garrison at Fort William, took matters into his own hands. He was supported by Lord Bury and Colonel Howard. Lord Bury, writing to

General Churchill on 26 May, urged the extirpation of the Stewarts of Appin as a clan. 'Surely the government can never have a better opportunity of rooting a rebellious clan out of the country, and peopling of it with those whose loyalty and zeal for the present royal family will be a terror to their neighbours.'

The inhuman and unlawful treatment of James of the Glen can only be ascribed to the fear, amounting to panic, throughout the country that rebellion would break out anew. It was only six years since the Battle of Culloden when the Stewarts of Appin had risen to fight for Prince Charles almost to a man. Their commander, Charles Stewart of Ardsheal, was an exile in France, but James was known to be sending his half-brother money and was certainly obedient to his word.

James became frantic during those first days of helpless inactivity while he lay in jail. We do not know if he and his sons (Charles was arrested later) were shackled in irons. His servants, nine of whom were held in custody, certainly were. James, beset with worries, seems to have almost lost his mind. Colonel Crawford, writing on 22 May, says, 'The prevarications and conduct of James Stewart appear to me every day blacker.'[1]

Three days before Crawford's comments, James had been allowed to write to a lawyer, Mr John Macfarlane, W.S. His letter, in which he actually names Allan Breck as the possible assassin, provides a clear indication of a man so desperate that he was on the point of naming Glenure's murderer, even though it was the same foster-son he had struggled to save.

He wrote that he and his son had been in prison on the grounds that they were:

[1] *Notable Scottish Trials*, p. 16.

'suspected to or knowing to the barbarous murder of Glenure . . . It is not pretended that I or my son were actors in this horrid action, as we both can be well attested; but alleges it was a premeditated thing, to which I must have been knowing: but so far otherwise, that no man (I thank God) abhors the fact more, and would if at liberty, do all in my power to bring it to light.

There is one Allan Stewart, a distant friend of the late Ardsheal's, who is in the French service, and came over in March last . . . and was, as I hear, the day the murder was committed, seen not far from the place where it happened . . . he is a desperate foolish fellow; and if he is guilty came to this country for that very purpose . . . I would own myself under many obligations to any friend would discover him: am persuaded he is gone south, in order to embrace the first opportunity of going abroad.'

He then goes on to explain why his mind is tormented:

'What makes my confinement very uneasy to me is, that this is the time of the year that my business would require my presence most; having bought cattle (wherein I yearly deal) in different countries, and taking grazings south for the cattle, which I must pay if I should never send a beast upon it; which I am afraid will be the case, if either my son or myself be not admitted to bail, to put our affairs in order: so hopes you'll spare no pains in this, as Airds and Appin will bail me to any sums whatever.'

Alas, despite this assurance, no concessions were made. Charles Stewart, the lawyer in Fort William whom John Beg MacColl had so desperately run to meet, turned out to be terrified for his own safety and failed James completely. Acharn was searched three times without a warrant. Visitors were forbidden and even his wife was not allowed to see him until the end of June. Eventually, on 6 July, seven weeks after his arrest, a warrant, dated 17 May, arrived at Fort William to order his detention.

After this he was at least allowed 'to take the air' in the prison, but his every movement was watched. He gave a shilling to the barber who came to shave him, asking him to hand it on to his servants, then lying in irons, with a message 'To say nothing but the truth, to keep their minds to themselves, and he would take care of them.' This was construed as bribery at his trial.

On 23 May, nine days after the murder, Captain David Chapeau, in General Pultney's foot regiment, was told by Campbell of Barcaldine (Glenure's half-brother) 'that there were some arms hid among the rocks near the panel's[2] house', so he went 'with a party, and took along with him Mr Patrick Campbell of Auchinsicallan, to direct him the road, and when they came to a hill above the panel's house [they] found the weapons which Dugald and John Beg MacColl had hidden – two muskets and four broad swords . . . the largest of the two fuzees was loaded, and the other not.'

Later, Captain Chapeau explained to the court that 'having drawn the shot of the loaded piece, he had found it to be loaded with small shot and it had appeared to him that the unloaded piece had been lately fired, having put his finger in the muzzle, which he had brought out black.'[3]

This was the gun which continually misfired for Allan Breck when he had tried to shoot blackcock. Its lock was attached by a single screw and tied to the stock with a piece of string. Idle as he was, Breck had probably forgotten to clean it,

[2] In Scots Law, a person indicted or accused of a crime is referred to as a 'panel' in court.

[3] From the evidence of Captain David Chapeau, *Notable Scottish Trials*, p. 175.

hence Captain Chapeau's dirty finger. However, the known inaccuracy of this weapon makes it virtually impossible that it could have been used to kill Glenure. Either Dugald and John Beg MacColl did not hide the weapons very well or Captain Chapeau and his men had been directed to them.

Two months later, in July, the bouman, who, claiming he had been threatened by the Stewarts, had actually asked to be arrested, came once more to the fore. He led Sergeant Baird and a party of soldiers from Fort William to the place where he had hidden Allan Breck's borrowed clothes. Sure enough the powder-horn, from which Breck had apparently concocted ink, was found in the pocket of the dark short coat.

John Stewart, 'young Ballachulish', a man of twenty-six who was also called *Iain Buidhe* because of his fair hair, became the champion of James. Regardless of his own safety, he went to Barcaldine Castle, demanding to see the copy of the arrest warrant. Barcaldine promptly refused, telling him to mind his own business. Persisting however, he went to Fort William and asked to see the original warrant, but Colonel Crawford, albeit with more civility, likewise refused his request.

The Campbells of Barcaldine, instigators of the private prosecution against all those connected with the murder of Colin Campbell of Glenure, demanded the arrest of both old Alexander Stewart of Ballachulish and his son. Sheriff Duncan Campbell, Barcaldine's brother, wanted Mrs MacDonald of Glencoe, Ardsheal's sister, 'taken up'. Mungo Campbell, Barcaldine's natural son and nephew of Glenure whom he had seen murdered, urged for the apprehension of young Fasnacloich, known to be Allan Breck's closest friend. He also demanded that 'all the tenants should be warned to remove, in the hopes that this threat would make them less reticent.'

However, despite the influence of Colin Campbell's relations, their demands for retribution did not materialise.

James of the Glen did have supporters in Edinburgh who raised an appeal on his behalf. They also procured an Edinburgh lawyer, Mr Stewart of Edinglassie, who promptly began organising his defence. On 20 August a warrant was issued by the Lord Justice Clerk to allow the prisoner's lawyers access to him in jail. The very next day, James was charged with aiding and abetting Allan Breck, while Allan himself was accused of the actual murder. The trial was fixed to take place in Inveraray on 21 of September.

Mr Stewart of Edinglassie went to Acharn to examine his client's papers but found that most had been removed during the three unwarranted searches which had been carried out. He began his journey back to Edinburgh, and by sheer good fortune, fell in with the party of soldiers who were escorting James of the Glen from Fort William to Inveraray. Somehow, he managed to persuade them to let him have a few words with his client by the roadside, and thus, for the first time since his arrest on 16 May, James was actually allowed to speak to a man who could legally defend his cause.

But time was desperately short. It was now 2 September and the following day the Gregorian Calendar was adopted in Great Britain, automatically changing the date to the 14th. James of the Glen would stand trial for his life within the space of a week.

James was held in the Tolbooth at Inveraray pending his trial. On 18 September, the Duke of Argyll refused James's counsel admittance and they had to wait until the next day before they were allowed to see the convicted man.

CHAPTER 12

The Trial of James Stewart

The Preliminary proceedings began on Thursday, 21 September. The trial was held in the old Kirk since the Tolbooth was too small.[1]

The case against James Stewart was brought jointly by private prosecutors acting on behalf of 'our lovit Janet Mackay . . . relict of the deceas'd Colin Campbell of Glenure and on behalf of Elizabeth and Lucy Campbells, her infant children,'[2] and by William Grant of Prestongrange, advocate for the Crown.

The three judges appointed were Lord Elchies, Sir James Ferguson of Kilkerran (both Lords of Justiciary) and, most importantly, the Lord Justice General, Archibald Campbell, 3rd Duke of Argyll.

The five counsel for the prosecution were the Lord Advocate, William Grant of Prestongrange; James Erskine, sheriff-depute of Perthshire; John Campbell, younger, of Levenside; Robert Campbell of Asnich; and Simon Fraser, Master of Lovat.

The inclusion of the latter must have raised some eyebrows

[1] From *Inveraray Notes* by Donald Mackechnie, p. 28.

[2] *Notable Scottish Trials*, p. 62.

for Fraser was the son of the notorious Lord Lovat, beheaded as a traitor after the Rising of 1745. Fraser had fought for the Jacobites but had found it expedient to swear loyalty to the Hanoverian king. The fact that he spoke Gaelic appears to have made him useful in this case and he seized the opportunity of vilifying James Stewart in order to ingratiate himself with Argyll. All of these men were paid by the private prosecutors, who were afterwards refunded by the Crown.

Counsel for the defence was headed by George Brown of Coalston, sheriff of Forfar, a lawyer of great experience who had been called to the bar in 1734; Thomas Miller, an advocate who was sheriff-depute of the Stewartry of Kirkcudbright; advocate Walter Stewart, younger, of Stewarthall; and finally Robert Macintosh, also an advocate and a well-known eccentric in his day.

From the forty-five men from Argyll and Bute cited to do service on the jury, fifteen were chosen. Much has been made of the fact that no less than eleven were Campbells. The likelihood of them being biased, not to say intimidated, by the presence of their chief *Mac Cailein Mor*, cannot be denied. Nonetheless, in fairness it must be pointed out that, at a time when the law demanded jurymen to be land-owners, few in these two counties did not bear the Campbell name.

Proceedings began with a proclamation being made at the instance of Glenure's widow, and also of his Majesty's advocate, against James Stewart of Acharn, in Duror, Appin, 'as guilty, actor or art and part of the crime of murder'. Allan Breck Stewart, 'being oft and diverse times called publicly by the macer of court, and thrice called at the outer door of the court house, to have compeared and underllyen the law for the crime of murder committed by him upon the said deceas'd Colin

Campbell of Glenure,' was then declared to 'be an outlaw and fugitive from his Majesty's laws' and ordained to 'be put to the horn'.[3]

Mr Walter Stewart, speaking for the defence, detailed the injustice of the treatment imposed upon James since the time of his arrest. Referring to his client's letter to Mr Macfarlane, W.S., in which he voiced his belief that Allan Breck was the murderer, the lawyer highlighted his client's honourable position. James, he argued, had wanted the murderer 'brought to justice; strange it is, indeed, to make this a crime! What should the panel have done? Should he have concealed the suspected murderer? No, my Lord, he acted a more honourable part, such a part as this Court will approve of, such a part that every member of it would have acted himself.'[4]

At this point, the Duke of Argyll interrupted angrily, denying that he 'or either of the other two judges, would have taken such a part'. On hearing this, James Stewart reputedly whispered to one of his agents: 'You may do for me what you will; but I know my fate by what the Duke of Argyll has just said to Mr Stewart.'

Walter Stewart was followed by Robert Macintosh, who again made a long speech in James's defence. Then it was the turn of Simon Fraser, appearing in his own words 'for Mrs Campbell of Glenure and her infant children'.

Fraser, having insisted that James had greatly resented Glenure's appointment as factor of the forfeited estates, declared that he had planned to kill him and had 'used his utmost endeavours to stir up some hot-headed ruffian to the execution of his plot'. He claimed that Allan Breck 'a man of desperate fortune' had shadowed Glenure before lying in wait to shoot him in the wood of Lettermore. He refuted the fact

[3] If a person was found guilty of a crime, the fact was proclaimed by a herald or a messenger at a public place, such as a town cross. Three blasts of a trumpet or horn were followed by the reading out of the proclamation for all to hear. If the trespasser failed to respond, 'letters of fire and sword' might be issued, and those to whom they were addressed would be required to put the accused to death.

[4] *Notable Scottish Trials*, pp. 72–3.]

that James had been denied his rights as a prisoner on the grounds that 'the military officers [were] unacquainted with the distinctions of the law.'[5]

Following him was Mr James Erskine, again acting for the prosecution. He announced quite blatantly that he was 'authorised to say that at Fort William the prisoner had many and great indulgences . . . he was allowed to take the air in the garrison, and to converse with his friends and relations . . . and, both before and since he was brought to this place, his agent and lawyers had had access to be with him as often as applied for in the proper way.' However, he did admit that the prisoner had not been allowed to see his servants and dependants 'from whom material evidence was expected . . . [and] who had declared that they were overawed by his authority'.[6]

The hypocrisy of the last statement must have been plain to at least a few in the courtroom who knew that James's servants had been held in irons, and threatened and bribed. John Beg MacColl is said to have been intimated by being thrown into the cell of a condemned man, to whom a minister was giving the last rights. Further, it was rumoured that someone else had concocted MacColl's evidence after drinking two bottles of whisky on the journey to Inveraray. Whatever the truth of these stories, it is highly probable that the evidence, if not wholly fabricated, had been tampered with.

Erskine was followed by the Lord Advocate, William Grant of Prestongrange, of whom it has been said that he acted with irreproachable integrity, except in the case of the trial of James of the Glen. The Petition to the Lord Justice Clerk to allow James's lawyers to see him in prison and the latter's agreement, dated 20 August, must have been known to him. Nonetheless, he too denied all knowledge of the hardships which James had

[5] Ibid, p. 92.

[6] Ibid, p. 102.

suffered since his arrest. Having detailed two other cases in which capital punishment resulted from circumstantial evidence, he went on to declare, 'My Lords, it appears to me that the present case affords a fresh instance, similar to those I have mentioned, of a providential discovery of circumstance serving to fix the guilt of accession to this murder upon the now panel.' [7]

Mr Thomas Miller, for the defence, then argued that this evidence was inconclusive. Much weight had been put upon the fact that James had supplied Allan Breck with money to escape. But Miller insisted that, 'The panel knew nothing of the place of Allan Breck's retreat until the day after the murder . . . if [his client] had been in concert with Allan Breck for several days before the commission of the murder . . . [he] would have had no difficulty to have furnished Allan Breck with a little money in order to make his escape immediately.' [8]

He concluded by pointing out that, according to the law of Scotland, the trial of James Stewart as an accessory 'cannot proceed until Allan Breck Stewart, the sole actor in the commission of the murder, is first tried and convicted'.

His case was not upheld. The Interlocator announced on behalf of the three judges that James Stewart was 'guilty, actor or art and part thereof, and therefore must stand trial'.

The Lords continued the 'diet' against James Stewart until 5 o'clock in the morning, when at last those within the court were allowed to go thankfully to bed and James was carried back to prison.

[7] Ibid, p. 116.

[8] Ibid, pp. 118–27.

The trial itself lasted for three days, from Friday, 22 September, to Sunday. It began with the prosecution taking evidence from the witnesses involved.

Colin Campbell of Glenure was murdered on Thursday, 14 May. Four days later, on Monday, Archibald Campbell of Stonefield, sheriff-depute of the shire of Argyll, then a man of fifty-six years old, travelled up to Appin to take evidence from anyone who might throw light on the crime. Some of those who testified, being actually suspected of the murder, were not put on oath immediately, so that they could be charged later if necessary. This also made it easier to bribe, threaten or otherwise pressure them to change their story.

Mungo Campbell was now factor of the forfeited estates and he seems to have changed his evidence deliberately to ensure revenge. When precognosced four days after the murder, he had said that on the hill he 'observed a man with a gun in his hand, cloathed . . . in a short dun-coloured coat and breeches of the same'.[9]

At the trial, however, when the short, black coat and long, blue-and-white striped trousers, which Allan had borrowed from James, were produced, he swore that the man he had seen was wearing 'a short, dark coat', with no mention of breeches at all.[10]

Thanks to Mungo's original statement, a man known as Red Ewan MacColl, brother of the bouman John Breck MacColl, had been arrested because his clothes (a dun-coloured jacket and breeches) matched the description of those the murderer had worn. In addition, it was well known that the bouman had the best gun in the district and was seen hiding such a weapon on the night after the murder. Despite this, Red

[9] From a copy of the *Precognitions* obtained by Lt. General Sir William MacArthur.

[10] From the evidence of Mungo Campbell; *Notable Scottish Trials*, p. 137.

Ewan was set free. His own humble station may have saved him when a scapegoat of greater importance could be had to demonstrate the fate of Jacobites who dared rebel.

When it came for James's servants to give evidence, Dugald, John Mor and John Beg MacColl told much the same story about the hiding of the swords and the two antiquated guns. John Beg explained how he had gone to Maryburgh with a letter from James to his lawyer, Charles Stewart, and had found him away from home. He also told of his meeting with the ferryman in the course of his journey home.

The evidence of little John, who had run so hard to Maryburgh on that fateful fourteenth day of May, does not, on the face of it, appear to incriminate James. Certainly, he told of the hiding of the illegal guns, but he also described their condition, which made it almost certain that neither was the weapon used to kill Glenure.

However, James himself cast doubt on the veracity of his servants' evidence. From the scaffold, minutes before he was due to be hanged, he told of how 'John Beg MacColl came in to the jail at Inveraray to see me next day after my sentence was passed, crying and tearing as if he was half-mad, and told me that the night Dougal MacColl and himself were on their way to [the trial at] Inveraray, at the Strath of Appin, Ewan Roy MacColl, portioner of Glassdrim, and the said John Mor MacColl, brought two bottles of *aqua vitae* into the barn, where they were confined, and wrought upon them to make up that story, and made them believe that it could not hurt me, and would gain them friendship at Barcaldine's hand.'[11]

He said that Alexander Stewart, the packman, had also lied, particularly about the amount of money which he had instructed the Maryburgh merchant, William Stewart, to give

[11] See *Appendix*, James Stewart's speech from the scaffold.

to Allan Breck. Their motives were clear to James. 'That there were plenty of bribes or rewards offered to several I am assured. Particularly Donald Ranken, herd to Ballachulish, a young boy, was offered eighteen hundred merks.'

However it was not the young herd boy (kept in prison so that none of the Stewarts could get near him) or any of his own servants who gave the damning evidence for which James was condemned to die.

Instead, it was the testimony of John Breck MacColl which dealt the fatal blow to James of the Glen's defence. It is known that the bouman had been threatened by what are described as 'the prisoner's friends' and had asked the Crown authorities to have him arrested.[12] From prison, he had led a party of soldiers to the cleft in the rock at Caolasnacoan where he had hidden the short, dark coat with the powder horn in the pocket and the striped trousers, borrowed by Allan Breck at Acharn.

The most important item of the prosecutor's case against James was the bouman's version of his meeting with Allan Breck. He swore on oath that Breck, having protested his innocence, had said that the family of Ardsheal would be suspected of the murder and, indeed, had gone so far as to say that James and his son Allan would doubtless be arrested. It was during this converstaion, so MacColl testified, that Allan Breck speculated as to whether the boy could hold his tongue, which 'was not so good as his father's'.

Today it seems barely conceivable that the word of an illiterate man, who was almost certainly bribed and intimidated, could be accepted by no less than three judges and a jury as unquestionable truth. Nonetheless, the bouman convinced them. He further embellished his story by describing how Allan, having written a letter with the

[12] *Trial of James Stewart*, p. 183.

sharpened end of a pigeon's feather, had asked him to take it to William Stewart to ask for enough money to enable him to get to France. The significance of this supposed credit, arranged by James with his cousin and brother-in-law the merchant, was construed by the prosecution to mean that a contingency escape plan for the murderer had been pre-arranged. Allan Breck would be given enough funds to flee the country should money not reach him by any other means.

Further to this statement the bouman, prodded by his wife, then elaborated on how, some two years before, when Glenure had first become the factor of Ardsheal Estate, mention had been made of how Ardsheal's children would suffer by the loss of a portion of the rents. He claimed that James of the Glen had then said that 'he would be willing to spend a shot upon Glenure, tho' he went upon his knees to his window to fire it'.[13] He added that he had heard 'that Ardsheal had sent home a message [saying] that he believed all his friends were dead, when Glenure was allowed to go on at the rate he did'.

James, who in his speech from the scaffold accused the bouman of lying,[14] said that he did not interrupt those who gave false witness against him for his lawyers had told him not to. They insisted that denial on his part would only provoke them into saying more.

The trial dragged on without a break from six o'clock on Friday morning until nearly eight on Sunday morning. At last, when all the witnesses for both the defence and prosecution had given their evidence, and letters from James Stewart, Colin of Glenure and others read out, the Lord Advocate, William Grant of Prestongrange, rose to address the jury.

He laid great emphasis on the evidence of John Breck MacColl the bouman, particularly in regard to the credit

[13] From the evidence of John Breck MacColl, *Notable Scottish Trials*, pp. 182–6.

[14] See *Appendix*.

which he claimed that James Stewart had arranged with his cousin William to give to Allan Breck. This, he said, could only have been done in the knowledge that Allan, whom he named as the murderer, would need money to escape.

He also insisted that the smaller of the two guns discovered in the moss above Acharn, the one with the lock tied on with string, had been the weapon used.

He was followed by the advocate, George Brown of Coalston, sheriff of Forfar, on behalf of James of the Glen. Brown denied the Lord Advocate's accusations, pointing out that there was no real proof that James of the Glen had made an arrangement, prior to the murder, to provide Allan Breck with money to leave the country, and he also asserted that the gun in question had a worn flint, rendering it virtually useless as a sporting gun, let alone accurate enough to kill a man. Brown spoke reasonably, but at such great length that an exhausted juryman, Campbell of Southhall, cried out, 'Pray, Sir, cut it short!'

When Sheriff Brown finally ended his address, the court was adjourned and the worn-out jurymen stumbled at last to their feet. The judges ordered them to give their verdict on the next day but in fact it was only some three hours later, at about eleven o'clock, when they declared their decision had been reached.

It was unanimous. James Stewart was found guilty of the murder of Colin Campbell of Glenure.

The Court then gave judgement, read out by the clerk, James Campbell, late Bailie of Inveraray who, on behalf of the Lord Justice-General, the Duke of Argyll, and the Lords Commissioners of Justiciary, ordered 'the said James Stewart to be carried back to the prison of Inveraray, and therein to

Archibald, 3rd Duke of
Argyll, in the robes of Lord
Justice General of Scotland
(painting by Allan Ramsay)

remain till the fifth day of October next, according to the
present stile, and then to be delivered over by the magistrates of
Inveraray and keeper of the said prison to the sheriff-depute of
Argyllshire . . . and delivered over to the sheriff-depute of
Inverness, and to then be transported to Fort William . . . to
remain until the 7th day of November next . . . and to then be
transported over the ferry of Ballachulish and delivered over to
the sheriff-depute of Argyllshire . . . and then carried to a
gibbet to be erected on a conspicuous eminence near the said
ferry; and . . . upon Wednesday the 8th day of November next,
betwixt the hours of twelve at noon and two afternoon, to be
hanged by the neck upon the said gibbet . . . until he be
dead.' [15]

[15] From the death
sentence read
out by James
Campbell, Clerk of
the Court, and
signed by the Duke
of Argyll, Lord
Elchies and Lord
Kilkerran.

Then the terrifying figure of the Duke of Argyll, the Lord-Justice General, bewigged and wearing robes of office, and towering above James of the Glen in his homespun clothes, brought the proceedings to a close. The taking of notes had been abandoned, all being too tired now to write. It was, however, remembered that the Duke began by telling the prisoner that he had had 'a most impartial trial' and that he had prosecuted 'with all the moderation consistent with the crime of which he stood accused'. He then harked back to the fact that the Stewarts of Appin had been rebels, fighting against the King in the Risings of 1715 and 1719 and more recently in 1745. His words had a clear message:

'I have thought it my duty to put you in mind of these facts, only to mark out those wicked paths which have led you to destruction . . . this murder has been visibly the effect and consequence of the late rebellion.

'You may yet during the short time you have to live, be of great service to your friends and neighbours by warning them against those principles and practices which have brought you to this untimely end; and may the Lord have mercy on your soul.' [16]

James of the Glen replied in simple words. 'My Lords, I tamely admit to my hard sentence. I forgive the jury and the witnesses who have sworn several things falsely against me, and I declare, before the great God and this auditory, that I had no previous knowledge of the murder of Colin Campbell of Glenure, and am as innocent of it as a child unborn. I am not afraid to die, but what grieves me is my character, that after ages should think me capable of such a horrid and barbarous murder.' [17]

The prisoner was then conducted to his cell.

[16] *Notable Scottish Trials*, p. 289.

[17] Ibid, p. 291.

The murder scene. A cairn was erected to mark the place where
Colin Campbell fell from his horse and died
(photograph by Gordon Ross Thomson)

A forestry track, leading from the
shore below, climbs deep into the
forest to reach the cairn which reads:
'This cairn is erected on the spot
where Colin Campbell of Glenure
was murdered on 14th May 1752'

Monument to James of the Glen on the south side of Ballachulish Bridge, marking the place where he was hanged. The stone on top, brought from his home at Acharn, is traditionally thought to be the very one on which he sat while watching his men at their work *(photograph by Malcolm MacGregor)*

The roofless Keil Chapel; wherein 'young Ballachulish' buried the bare, washed bones of James of the Glen, laying them beside the body of his dead wife, Margaret Stewart

CHAPTER 13

The Execution

James of the Glen was hanged on 8 November 1752. A
scaffold, erected on *Cnap a'Cholais*, a knoll just above the
south end of the Ballachulish Bridge, had been specially
strengthened with iron. The site is marked by a monument,
surmounted by the very rock on which James had sat and
supervised his men when they were working in the fields at
Acharn. It provides a fitting memorial to a farmer, imbued
with a love of the land.

A letter in the *Journal* of Bishop Forbes (author of *The Lyon
in Mourning*) indicates how James Stewart was venerated a
generation after his death. The Bishop relates 'that a gentleman
of the name of Cameron charitably visited James Stewart when
prisoner in Fort William, after sentence of death had been
pronounced, and generously offered to rescue him with fifty
men only from the command that might be appointed to guard
him to his place of execution, which proposal, equally friendly
and courageous, James as generously refused, alleging that such
an attempt would no doubt be attended with more hurt to his
country than his life was worth, and therefore expressly desired

such a thing might never be mentioned again.

'The spot where the attempt was to have been made was pointed out to me, and from its situation I'm fully persuaded it could have succeeded, especially as the day proved most tempestuous and rainy, and poisoned the muskets of the party – two companies – so that they could not have been discharged. Besides, the poor sogers, greatly sympathising with the prisoner, looked for some such attempt, and were determined to make only a sham resistance against any attack.' [1]

As the bishop notes, the day of James's execution was one of gales and torrential rain. Two ministers prayed with him and gave him the last rites within the shelter of a tent. Then the condemned man read aloud his 'Dying Speech'. [2]

In this, having first described the injustice done to him both before and during his trial, he denied with great emphasis that he had been in any way involved in Glenure's murder and adamantly declared 'nor do I know who was the actor'. He prayed that God would forgive the jury and the witnesses, who had lied against him, and said that he died a true member of the Episcopalian Church. He concluded by saying that he was sorry if he had asserted anything that was not true.

After this he knelt down and read aloud Psalm 35, which to this day is known throughout the Highlands as *'Salm Seumas a' Ghlinne'*.

[1] from the *Journal* of Bishop Forbes, p. 305.

[2] For the complete speech, as read from the foot of the scaffold, see Appendix.

[3] Verses 21-23.

They gaped upon me with their mouths,
and said: fie on thee, fie on thee, we saw it with our eyes.
This thou hast seen, O Lord: hold not thy tongue then,
go not far from me, O Lord.
Awake, and stand up to judge my quarrel:
avenge thou my cause, my God, and my Lord. [3]

Then, having said goodbye to his friends, 'he mounted the ladder with great courage and resolution, and read a short written prayer with an audible voice.'

Following his death, the body of James of the Glen was hanged in chains from the gibbet: a sinister warning of the penalty of defying the law. Fifteen soldiers were sent to prevent it from being removed.

The guard was still present in 1755, when the body was blown down in a gale. The skeleton was wired up until, one by one, each bone fell to the earth. Young Ballachulish (now the laird), faithful to the last, collected them. His daughter, a little girl of ten, actually washed the skull. Then, placing them in the coffin which contained the remains of Margaret Stewart, he buried husband and wife in the grounds of Keil Chapel.

The gibbet itself was eventually thrown into the sea from *Boinne na Gibbet* – the rocks below the stanchion of the Ballachulish Bridge on the Appin shore. A local boy, dubbed *Mac a Phì a chutaich* ('MacPhee of the madness or simple mindedness') was blamed, but nothing was done to punish him, presumably for lack of proof. According to legend, the wood was carried by the tide down Loch Linnhe and was eventually washed up on the north shore of Loch Etive, where some say it was made into a bridge and others into part of a pew in Ardchattan Church. Whatever the truth of these stories, the local people, sickened by the sight of it, were thankful to see it disappear.

CHAPTER 14

Who Fired the Fatal Shot?

T he identity of the murderer of Colin Campbell of
Glenure has long remained a mystery. In the midst of
all the gossip, intrigue and false testimony, two
important facts emerge from the records of the trial and the
happenings thereafter. Firstly, James of the Glen, although
denying all knowledge, must have had a fair idea of who had
killed the factor. Secondly, from the moment of James's arrest,
it appears that young Ballachulish lived in an agony of mind.

James of the Glen must have been shielding someone,
someone for whom he was prepared to die. Who could it have
been? Apart from Allan Breck, his own sons, particularly the
eldest, Allan, are prime suspects.

On 5 May, 1753, John Campbell of Achallader, factor to
Breadalbane, wrote as follows to his brother-in-law John
Campbell of Barcaldine:

*We hear from Balquhidder that Robin Oig is returned in good
plight to that country . . . he gives out – at least it is given out
in his name – that he saw Breck in France who got there in*

March, and who says it was Allan Beg that actually committed the murder; and that Breck is to publish a vindication of himself.

A letter from Colonel John Crawford, commander of the garrison at Fort William, to John Campbell of Glenure, undated but obviously written in 1752, reads:

> *I beg that in your writing to Inveraray these three questions may be put to Dugald MacColl and inserted in his precognitions.*
>
> *1st, as to having seen Allan Breck in ye brewhouse handling one of his master's guns and complaining of the locks.*
>
> *2nd, the time he saw young Allan going with Laggan How [a tenant of the farm of that name below Beinn a Bheithir] towards the wood on the day of the murder; and*
>
> *3rd, that both MacColls shou'd be strongly dealt with as to the conversation mention'd by Dun. Roy [James Mor MacGregor] in the prison and the causes for pitying young Allan, and why they thought he would be hang'd as well as his Fayr.*

When questioned, however, the MacColls did not incriminate Allan, who was able to prove that both he and his brother Charles had been at Fasnacloich, in Glen Creran, some four miles away from the wood of Lettermore, all afternoon on the 14 May. They had gone there 'after dinner' (which was usually about noon), escorting their sister Elizabeth and her friend Mary Stewart, daughter of 'old Fasnacloich', who had been staying at Acharn. Both Allan and Charles were arrested and imprisoned, but nothing could be proved against them in connection with Colin Campbell's death.

'They all knew that James Stewart of Glen Duror was innocent, and also if they tried to save him at the expense of him who they knew to have done the deed, he would be the one to resent it,' so wrote Mrs Mary Mackellar, a Lochaber lady, in a letter to the *Oban Times* in 1890.[1]

So if it was not one of his own sons, who did James die to save?

At a wild guess it could have been his chief. Dugald Stewart, 10th of Appin, is a man of whom little is known. He had refused to rise for Prince Charles in 1745 and Charles Stewart of Ardsheal, who had commanded the Appin Regiment in his place, was now exiled abroad. Is it therefore possible that by killing the Crown factor Dugald was trying to regain the respect of his clan? Young Ballachulish had been with him at Lettershuna (now Appin House) on the fateful Thursday, 14 May. Reputedly, hearing of the murder on his way home, Ballachulish wheeled round his horse and rode back to Lettershuna to break the news to his chief. Admittedly, the theory of Appin's involvement is far fetched, but it could account for the way in which young Ballachulish subsequently behaved. First, he risked being taken prisoner himself by going to the Black Castle of Barcaldine and then to Fort William demanding to see the warrant for James's arrest. Then, according to local legend, his family is said to have roped him to his bed on the day of the hanging to prevent him telling what he knew. James of the Glen had been convicted and it was too late to prevent his death, they told him. He would jeopardise his own life.

Much the same story is told of Donald Stewart, John's first cousin, who is said to have had to be 'restrained' at the time of the execution. Donald, who had been wounded at Culloden,

[1] *Oban Times*, 28th June, 1890.

had been given a home by his uncle, old Ballachulish, for whom he worked on the farm. General MacArthur[2] claims that Donald could not have been the murderer because the men working with him would have noticed his disappearance at the time when the shot was fired.

However, with their laird waiting for the factor and his son away with the chief, what is more likely than the men took time off to work on their own bits of land? Donald was a young man. He could have run up the hill, killed Glenure and been down again before Kennedy, the sheriff's officer, appeared crying for help. The gun which was found later hidden in a tree – reputedly in the old yew by Ballachulish House – could have been the one used to kill Glenure. It is claimed that old Ballachulish told the girl who discovered it that 'it was the gun of misfortune'.

Donald is the subject of a well-known legend which tells how some local men had gathered at a place called *Lagan Bhlàr an Lochain*, high up in the hills to the south of Salachan Glen, from where no gunshot could be heard. They agreed that 'whoever had the best gun should hand it over for a certain purpose; and whoever was the best shot should do the deed.'

On the appointed day, they met and tested the guns, 'and it was a gun belonging to a man called Dugald MacColl (known by the name of Dugald of the Locks) that was the best gun for firing bullets. If a bullet and a chaser were put into it, it would fire the two so straight that they would not be an inch from each other in the mark in the target. And it was a man called Donald, son of Donald, brother's son to the Laird of Ballachulish, who was the man with the best eye for marksmanship. Dugald of the Lock's gun was given to Donald Stewart, and he was to go with the object of killing Glenure.

[2] In his book *The Appin Murder*, p. 101.

The Laird of Fasnacloich was another who was chosen on account of his skill with the gun, and he was chosen for the same business.'

Another story tells of when Alexander Campbell of Barcaldine (brother of Glenure) went stalking with Donald Stewart on the Moor of Rannoch. Apparently, Donald shot a stag at an amazing range with his long-barrelled gun, called a *t-slinneanach*.[3]

Reaching the dead beast, they found that it had been 'struck behind the shoulder, and the bullet and the chaser were only about two breadths from each other. Alexander, seeing this, said, "That is exactly the way in which Colin, my brother was struck; and I am much mistaken if that is not the very gun which did the deed, whatever the hand which held it."

'Donald Stewart asked him, "Do you think it was I that killed your brother?" to which Alexander replied, "No." [However] that talk occasioned a coolness between the two, and each of them went his own way home.'

The story concludes: 'Donald Stewart went to sea, and he returned no more.'[4]

The Laird of Fasnacloich, whose skill with the gun made him suitable 'for the same business', which we can assume to be the killing of Glenure, is generally taken to be James Stewart, or young Fasnacloich; his father by that time being an old man of about sixty-six. James, who was twenty-nine in 1752, had been wounded at Culloden and knew the awful, gruesome truth of how survivors of the battle had been wantonly killed. He may have nursed a personal hatred for Colin Campbell, who supposedly betrayed prisoners at Aberdeen. James's close association with Allan Breck resulted in a warrant being taken out for his arrest. However, the fact

[3] The Gaelic *slinneanach* means 'shoulder' or 'shoulder blade', so the word *t-slinneanach* implies that this was a heavy gun that had to be fired from the shoulder.

[4] From the *Transactions of the Gaelic Society of Inverness*, 'The Appin Murder', p. 387.

that he was proved to have been at a meeting at Tigh-phuirt, in Glencoe, at the precise time when Colin Campbell was shot, served to clear his name.

The meeting in question was in the change-house or inn at Tigh-phuirt. The chairman appears to have been MacDonald of Glencoe, who, as the group's cattle-dealing business drew to a close, providentially, and it would seem purposefully, looked at his watch and proclaimed that it was then 'between six and seven o'clock'.

Tigh-phuirt is about five miles from the place where Colin Campbell was shot between five and half-past five. It was noted at the meeting that Red Ewan MacColl (brother of John Breck the bouman) arrived only about an hour before Glencoe looked at his timepiece. Therefore, it is just possible that MacColl, a fleet-footed Highlander, could have shot Glenure and reached Tigh-phuirt within an hour. His clothes, a short dun coat and breeches, were such as described originally by Mungo, Colin's nephew, who saw the killer running away. Furthermore, Ewan is known to have possessed a good gun. Despite this, however, Ewan was released after questioning and then summoned as a witness at the trial, where, together with his brother the bouman, he gave false testimony against James Stewart of the Glen. In this light, the reasons behind why the bouman provided such damning evidence against James Stewart become more understandable.

Is it actually possible that old Fasnacloich, claimed by historians to be too old to be of significance, organised the killing of Glenure? He is known to have quarrelled with John Campbell of Barcaldine over a lease of land near Loch Etive. Fasnacloich had evicted the Campbells in favour of a MacLaren who paid him a higher rent.[5] According to *The Traditional*

[5] Ibid, vol. XXXV, p. 374.

Account taken from John F. Campbell's MSS of *West Highland Tales*, the laird of Fasnacloich had leased Campbell land to some MacLarens who were related to the Stewarts. Colin of Glenure was so incensed by this that he threatened to ensure that 'not a clod of the land of Appin would be possessed by a Stewart, nor a clod of the land of Lochaber possessed by a Cameron'.[6] Old Fasnacloich is reported to have been seen going to the hill on the morning of the day of the murder, carrying a gun. The alliance between the Stewarts and MacLarens was strong: it had begun with the marriage of John Stewart of Lorn to the daughter of MacLaren of Ardveich in 1463 and had continued for nearly two hundred years. Was old Fasnacloich obeying an age-old blood tie by giving this gun to MacLaren to kill Glenure?

Old Fasnacloich had been saved by a man called Donald MacIntyre, who was brought before the sheriff and asked whether he had seen 'the Laird of Fasnacloich under arms on the day on which Glenure was killed'. Donald MacIntyre said that he had not, and since he was the only witness, they had to set Fasnacloich free.

Some time later Fasnacloich came across MacIntyre working in a field and said to him, 'I am much obliged to you for having perjured yourself at Inveraray to save me.'

'Devil take you, do you say that I perjured myself for your sake?' came the reply.

'Tell me then, Donald, how do you clear yourself?' asked Fasnacloich, to which Donald returned: 'I was asked if I had seen the Laird of Fasnacloich on the day before the night on which Colin of Glenure was killed, taking to the hill under arms, I said that I had not. I saw only one gun in your possession and you know yourself it would take two to make arms.'

[6] Ibid, vol. XXXV, p. 374.

Thus, according to legend, was Fasnacloich saved from death by an illiterate Highlander's sagacity and quickness of mind.

Some historians name Robin Oig, son of Rob Roy MacGregor, as the assassin. Initially, this seems most unlikely. The MacGregors had long been at enmity with the MacLarens, supporters of Clan Stewart of Appin since the fifteenth century. In addition, it seems beyond comprehension that James of the Glen would sacrifice his own life for a man with a criminal record, and a man with whom, as far as it is known, he had no previous connections. Some people, however, believed then as today that Robin Oig, who had already murdered a MacLaren in Balquhidder in a remarkably similar way, was hired to kill Glenure. The two crimes were almost identical. Both men were shot in the back with a long-barrelled Spanish gun. Robin Oig owned such a weapon and, outlawed as he was for the MacLaren murder, he would certainly have been desperate enough to earn money to escape abroad. As has been stated, his brother, too, was in dire straits and would have had nothing to lose by becoming embroiled in the affair.

The following memorial sent by John Campbell of Barcaldine, Glenure's half-brother, to the Barons of the Exchequer in July or August 1752, is remarkable.

I am informed that James Stewart in Acharn . . . when in this town in April last about getting a suspension of the Decreets of Removal, at Glenure's instance against the tenants of Ardsheal, did visit James Drummond, alias MacGregor, prisoner in the Tolbooth . . . and did propose to him a scheme of disabling Glenure from acting as factor upon the forfeited estates. What he proposed was that James Drummond should give to him, James Stewart, a letter directed to Robert Campbell, alias MacGregor, brother to the said James Drummond (a person under sentence of fugitation) desiring the said Robert to do whatever the said James Stewart desired him, particularly to murder Glenure, for which purpose the said James Stewart was to furnish a very good gun. James Drummond's bribe was to get a prorogation of a Beneficial Tack [lease] he then enjoyed from a near relation to whom he was Tutor; the bribe to Robert was James Stewart's affording him money to carry him to ffrance, where by Ardsheal's interest he was to get a Commission in the ffrench service, or a pensione, whichever he chused.[7]

The Barons forwarded this epistle to Mr Pelham, Chancellor of the Exchequer, with the request that James Mor Drummond should receive a pardon to allow him to appear as a witness at the trial of James Stewart. The petition, however, was refused on the grounds that 'there will not be time sufficient before the tryal of James Stewart to apply to His Majesty for his royal pardon in order to capacitate James Drummond to give evidence upon that occasion altho' the circumstances had been more strong and perswasive to make their Excellencies imagine that the testimony of the one would materially tend to the conviction of the other.'

James Stewart, when about to die on the scaffold, positively denied involvement with James Mor Drummond, a man notorious as a rogue. Indeed, circumstances point to it being Allan Breck, rather than James, who somehow got access to the prison where he promised to reward both Rob Roy's sons for the murder of Glenure.[8] Allan Breck is known to have been in

Edinburgh in February 1752, shortly after landing at Leith from France. As usual, he left the capital owing money. His foster-father, James, had to settle his debt with Hugh Stewart, owner of the lodging-house near the Fountain's Well in the Royal Mile. In this scenario, presuming Robin Oig was the marksman, he could not have found the perfect place to lie in wait for his victim without the aid of someone familiar with the ground. The theory that several men in Appin conspired to kill Glenure, so loudly voiced at the time, seems valid in the present day. Therefore, it appears that it was an accomplice, rather than the man who actually pulled the trigger, that James Stewart, through his silence, saved.

James Mor Drummond, in the pretence of a cobbler, escaped from prison with his daughter's connivance just before he was due to be hanged. Having reached Dunkirk, France, Drummond wrote to Campbell of Barcaldine on 12 June 1753 with news that Allan Breck had been 'sent over to murder your brother and money given to him for that purpose'.[9]

He asks for a warrant authorising Allan's arrest declaring, 'I shall go to any length to serve you,' before revealing the true purpose of the letter 'but as I am but poor it cannot be supposed I can go throw with this unless I get some cash or a bill to support the carrying on of this affair.'

Plainly desperate for money, he was willing to betray a former friend. But could he have had another motive, such as getting his revenge for a promise of payment unfulfilled?

Sir Walter Scott, in his introduction to *Rob Roy*, affirms that Allan Breck and James Mor were 'as thick as thieves' before the latter tried to betray his former friend. The novelist describes how 'MacGregor stipulated for a licence to return to England, promising to bring Allan Breck thither along with him. But

[9] From *The Trial of James Stewart*, Appendix XVI, p. 364.

the intended victim was put on his guard by two countrymen, who suspected James's intentions towards him. He escaped from his kidnapper, after, as MacGregor alleged, robbing his portmanteau of some clothes and four snuff-boxes. Such a charge, it may be observed, could scarce have been made unless the parties had been living on a footing of intimacy, and had access to each other's baggage.' [10]

The belief that Robin Oig was the 'hit man' was plainly that of an old man in Balquhidder, now dead some eighty years. Recalling the Appin Murder, he always claimed that 'justice was done in the end' – Robin Oig was finally caught and hanged for the abduction of the widow Jean Key in 1754. And the inference becomes clear when one remembers that, of all those involved in the murder of Glenure, whether by involvement or association, only he and James Stewart were put to death.

A local Appin legend, relating to the 'suicide's grave', casts the net of involvement and of retribution even wider. A simple stone cross, behind the Scottish Episcopal Church of St Mary's, Ballachulish, is claimed to commemorate a man who threw himself to his death from the roof of Ballachulish House. Traditionally, this tragedy is linked the Appin Murder. In fact, the cross is inscribed with the names of Charles 'Stuart' [sic] of Ballachulish and his son, Henry, who died, apparently within a short time of each other in 1875 – one hundred and twenty-three years after Colin Campbell was killed.

The family papers state that Charles Stewart, the 7th laird, died in 1875, leaving sons called Dugald and John. There is no mention of his other son, Henry. Was this because Henry had already committed suicide? Legend has it that the shame of knowing their family's involvement in the murder, and in the hanging of an innocent man, drove him to kill himself, but so much time had passed between the two events that this seems very unlikely.

What is true is that Charles Stewart was the son of Lilias, the little girl who washed the skull of James of the Glen when she was only ten. Her father, John, buried the skull and other bones within the ruined chapel of Keil.

The Pre-Reformation chapel, now roofless, stands above Loch Linnhe; a lonely and lovely place where, on a windless day, one hears only the cawing of rooks and the ceaseless murmur of the sea. Within the church itself several graves are overgrown but that of James of the Glen, on the south-east side against the wall, remains, as he long ago prophesied, entirely bare of grass.

Plaque marking the burial place of James of the Glen in churchyard of Keil Chapel. Grass does not, and never has, grown on his grave.

EPILOGUE

In 1787, Alexander Campbell of Ardchattan wrote to his father from Paris telling him of his adventures in the capital of pre-Revolutionary France. He described how he had been dining in an inn when 'a tall, thin man' came in, claiming to be Allan Breck'.

The tone of his letter implies that, although not convinced of his identity, Campbell believed the stranger to be from Scotland and for this reason listened to what he had to say. Doubtless he also gave him a drink and some food for which, from his description, he may have been in need. The man, who may have been Breck, spoke of the by then notorious 'Appin Murder' and swore that he had not killed Glenure.

Then he walked out into the Paris street and vanished, just as he had done so many years before in the darkness before dawn in Glencoe.[1]

[1] From information given by Alastair Campbell of Airds, Unicorn Pursuivant.

The Speech of James Stewart from the Scaffold

My dear countrymen,

The several motives that induced me to offer to the world a narrative of my uncommon misfortunes are as follows:

First of all, my innocence makes my sufferings easy, and alleviates all afflictions, be they never so severe in the eyes of man.

Secondly, that my silence upon this occasion might not be constructed to my prejudice by my prosecutors, as my silence at the bar, when I was hearing some of the evidence ever untruths against me, was said to have proceeded from conviction of guilt, and that if I should challenge them they would say more than they did.

Thirdly, in order to let the world know the hardships put upon me since my confinement, contrary to the known laws of this nation, which effectually disabled me from making many defences I otherwise might produce.

Fourthly, that it came to my ears my prosecutors had spread a false report that I made a confession of that crime when in Inveraray gaol after receiving my hard sentence.

Fifthly, that I might offer my public advice to my friends and relations upon this melancholy occasion.

These are the chief reasons for the following narration of facts, which I did hope to make appear so clear as will convince the unprejudiced part of mankind how much I am injured, and that I die, as

I endeavoured to live, an honest man.

As to the first article, of my being art and part accessary to Glenure's murder, I positively deny, directly or indirectly, nor do I know who was the actor, further than my suspicion of Allan Breck Stewart, founded upon circumstances that have cast up since the murder happened; and I do declare that it was not from any conviction of his being guilty of that crime I sent him money to carry him off the country, but out of charity and friendship I had for him, not only as a relation, but likewise as a pupil left to my charge by his father, and as a person who kept close to my brother in his greatest distress when lurking, before he got off the country; and that I knew he was a deserter, so durst not stand a precognition. I also declare it was without my knowledge he carried any part of my clothes with him from my house upon the Tuesday before the murder; nor did I know where he was or where he had gone to from that time, until Donald Stewart, nephew to Ballachulish, came to me Friday after that unlucky action happened, and told Allan Breck was at Caolasnacoan, and begged I might send him some money to help him off the country, for fear of being secured for the above reason of his being a deserter; and the said Donald Stewart told me that Allan Breck assured him he had no hand in the murder.

I likewise declare, though it is set forth in my indictment that Allan Breck frequented my house and company most of any place since he came to this country in March last, that I did not see him but thrice from his coming till he went away from the country. The first time was two nights before I went to Edinburgh in the beginning of April last. The next, or second, time was about eight days after my return from Edinburgh, which was about the last days of April, as I best remember, when he stayed but one night when I was at home. The third and last time was upon the Monday before Glenure's murder, that he came to my house about one of the clock afternoon, and stayed that night; and the next morning I went from home, which was Tuesday, before he was out of bed, nor did I see him that day or since. Nor can I remember Glenure's name was spoken of in his company either of the last two times, unless it was he that told me Glenure was gone for Lochaber upon the Monday, as to which I cannot be positive; but I am very sure there was no word of destroying him in any way spoke of. The first time he must have heard me talk of Glenure, as I told him I was going to give in a Memorial for the tenants to the Barons of Exchequer.

It is also set forth in my indictment that it was of my own accord, and not at the desire of the tenants, I went to make application for them in law. I do declare it was their desire that all lawful ways should be taken to keep them in possession, and do assure myself that nothing obliged them to refuse that, but fear and ignorance, believing that if they should own it they would be made prisoners, as all the poor people were put in such a terror by a military force kept in different parts of the country, that they – I mean the poor country people – would say whatever they thought pleased my prosecutors best.

I declare what John Dow Breck MacColl, bouman in Caolasnacoan, deponed in regard to my coming to Glenure's window was false, and that at the time he condescended on I should have said so, being two years ago, I was in very good friendship with Glenure, which his letters to me about that time testify.

As to the story John Mor MacColl, Dougal MacColl, and John Beg MacColl, my servants, told they heard me say in my brewhouse, that if Glenure did live five years he would be laird of Appin, and that I saw people in Appin that would not allow Glenure to go at such a rate, this I do not remember. But this I can safely say, that John Beg MacColl came into the gaol at Inveraray to see me next day after my sentence was passed, crying and tearing as if he was half mad, and told me that the night Dougal MacColl and he himself were on their way to Inveraray, at the strath of Appin, Ewan Roy MacColl, portioner of Glassdrim, and the said John Mor MacColl, brought two bottles of aqua vitae into the barn where they were confined, and wrought upon them to make up that story, and made them believe that it could not hurt me, and would gain them friendship at Barcaldine's hand. I truly believe, though, it were the truth that it could not hurt any other person, though anything was proof enough against a man so ill looked upon as I seemed to be.

Alexander Stewart, packman, deponed several falsehoods, particularly in regard of the five guineas he said I desired him to tell William Stewart, merchant in Maryburgh, to give John Dow Breck credit in for Allan Breck's use, and his saying I desired him to get only four pounds sterling from William Stewart for paying milk cows bought for his use at Ardsheal, whereas he was only desired to get eight pounds sterling for paying these cows, as they in truth were bought for William Stewart's use.

I declare the reason why I did not challenge them at the bar was that my lawyers desired me, though I heard a witness swear falsely, not to speak, otherwise I should be the worse looked upon; so that I hope the unbiased will believe that my silence did not proceed from fear, as alleged by my enemies, but in obedience to the advice given to me by my counsel, which I was determined to follow whatever should happen.

That there were plenty of bribes or rewards offered to several I am assured. Particularly Donald Ranken, herd to Ballachulish, a young boy, was offered eighteen hundred merks, which are his own words, but he was kept close prisoner at Inveraray, so that none of my friends had access to put any question to him. John Maccombich, late miller in the mill of Ardsheal, was offered his former possession of the mill for telling anything would answer their turn. Duncan Maccombich and Duncan MacColl, both in Lagnaha, were offered as much meal as they pleased to call for at Fort William if they would make any discoveries.

I now leave the world to judge what chance a man had for his life when such bribes were offered to poor, ignorant, country people, or what assurance can any man have but such bribes prevailed with some of those who did make oath.

As to the uncommon hardships put upon me under my confinement they were many, such as being taken into custody without any written warrant on the 16th day of May last; carried through night to Fort William, where I was kept close prisoner; not allowed to see any of my friends, or any that could give me counsel, until about the 20th of June there came a letter from Mr William Wilson, directed to my wife, with the Act of Parliament discharging close imprisonment longer than eight days, which, when shown to Colonel Crawford, who then commanded the fort and troops, he allowed my wife and some others to see me, but would not allow such as I thought could be of most use to me to come near me, particularly Mr Stewart, younger of Ballachulish, who came with some law advices to me, would not be admitted; nor would Charles Stewart, writer, or William Stewart, merchant, Maryburgh, get any admittance. In short any who could be supposed to be of any service to me in making my defences were not permitted access to me. I do not impute this usage to Colonel Crawford, for whom I retain a very great regard, and who did not want humanity, had he not got a very bad impression of me from my prejudiced persecutors. And when Colonel Crawford left Fort William some time in the beginning of July, the new governor would allow none to come near me, turned my wife twice from the fort and discharged her to stay at Maryburgh.

And in that close situation was I kept, until my indictment came to hand about the latter end of August; so had no way to make up my defences, nor durst any of my friends in the country offer to do for me, otherwise they would be laid up prisoners; and those who I expected had most to say for my exculpation were taken prisoners, and kept close till my trial, so had not access to put any questions to them, by which they were not ready to make their answers when called at the bar. I am far from charging the governor with this hard usage, who appears to be a good-natured man, but had his orders so to use me.

When my trial came on I found it was not only Glenure's murder I had to answer for, of which I thank God my conscience could easily clear me, but the sins and follies of my forefathers were charged against me, such as the Rebellion in 1715, in 1719, and 1745, so could not be allowed the character of an honest man; notwithstanding that, I firmly believe there was none present but who was either himself, or came of people that were, concerned in rebellion some time or other. God forbid that they should be all called villains upon that account, as the greatest sinner, upon his repenting, may turn saint.

I was a schoolboy in the year 1715, and was but little more in the year 1719; and if I had the misfortune to be concerned in the year 1745, I was indemnified, and have done nothing since to incur the Government's displeasure that I am conscious of.

Another surprising charge against a man in a Christian country came in against me, which was that I was a common parent to fatherless children, and took care of widows in the country, which gained me great influence over the people, by which they were much led by me - or some words to that purpose. I hope soon to appear before a Judge who will reward charity and benevolence in a different way; and I only regret how little service was in my power to do, not only to the fatherless and widows, but to all mankind in general, as I thank God I would make all the race of Adam happy if I could.

Another charge, and a heavy one, was that when sub-factor to Glenure I exacted more rents of the tenants than were paid to the Exchequer, and which superplus rents I wrongously applied, either to my own use or to the behoof of my brother Ardsheal's children.

I own I did get some acknowledgments from some of the tenants, with the knowledge and consent of the factor, Glenure; and do declare that I was as assiduous as in my power in acting for the benefit of said children, and that I did account for their behoof for all I could make of those lands over and above the rent paid to the factor, and thought it no crime to do so, but, to the contrary, thought it my duty, to which I was bound by the ties, not only of nature, but also of gratitude, being the distressed offspring of a very affectionate, loving brother, to whom I was under many obligations, and whose misfortunes, I am well assured, proceeded from a conviction of his doing his duty, which may be construed by some to be owing to the prejudice of his education.

I do declare that I made no confession of the crime alleged against me at Inveraray or elsewhere, and that I had it not to make. Nor can I remember that any there asked me the question, excepting Mr Alexander Campbell, minister, who, I am persuaded, could not be capable of being author of that false calumny, which must have been raised by some malicious persons. May God forgive them. It is very true that I told Mr Campbell I had no personal love for Glenure, and that I was sorry how few in his neighbourhood had. But I hope no man would construct that as if I had an intention to murder him.

I also told him that I had the charity to believe that the bulk of the jury thought I had some foreknowledge of the murder. Yet I still think, and not without some reason, that they gave themselves too little time to consider the proofs of either side, but gave in their verdict upon the presupposed notion of guilt. What must convince all well-thinking people of their being so prepossessed is their stopping one of my lawyers twice in his speech to them after the witnesses were examined. Mr Campbell of Southhall, if I noticed right, was the first that interrupted my lawyer. There was some other who also spoke, and who I did not know. I am told this is not often practised in Christian countries, but there are many ways taken upon some emergencies for answering a turn, and it appears I must have been made a sacrifice, whoever was guilty.

As to what Alexander Campbell in Tayinluib deponed, that I did not know what I should help any of his name to if it was not to the gallows, I do remember part of what passed, though my memory is not quite so good as Mr Campbell's or Colin MacLaren's; but this far I can safely say, upon the word of a Christian going into eternity, that I had no other intention in what I said than a joke; and that if I had any grudge at himself for being Campbell, I was under no necessity to go into his house, as there was another public-house within a gunshot of his door.

As to what Ewan Murray and Colin MacLaren deponed in regard to my telling them that I had given a challenge to Glenure, I own I was wrong in telling them that story, as it was a thing they had no concern in.

And as to what Colin MacLaren deponed I should have said upon the road after parting with Ewan Murray, I solemnly swear I do not remember one word that passed being much the worse of liquor, as he himself owned upon oath.

I do declare that I frankly forgive all these evidences and jury as freely as I want forgiveness for my sins, and do from my heart pray that God may pardon them and bring them to a timeous repentance, and that they may not be charged with my innocent blood, as I never intended any of them the least harm.

My dearest friends and relations, I earnestly recommend and entreat you, for God's sake, that you bear no grudge hatred, or malice to those people, both evidence and jury, who have been the means of this, my fatal end. Rather pity them, and pray for them, as they have my blood to answer for. And though you hear my prosecutors load my character with the greatest calumny, bear it patiently, and satisfy yourselves with your own conviction of my innocence. And may this my hard fate put an end to all discord among you, and may you all be united by brotherly love and charity. And may the great God protect you all, and guide you in the ways of peace and concord, and grant us a joyful meeting at the great day of judgment.

I remember Mr Alexander Campbell, minister of Inveraray, for whom I have a great value for his kind and good advices, told me that the fear of discovering any of my friends might be a temptation to me from making my confession of my knowledge of that murder.

Therefore, to do my friends justice, so far as I know, I do declare that none of my friends, to my knowledge ever did plot or concert that murder; and I am persuaded they never employed any person to accomplish that cowardly action; and I firmly believe there is none of my friends who might have a quarrel with that gentleman but had the honour and resolution to offer him a fairer chance for his life than to shoot him privately from a bush.

Mr Brown of Coalston, Mr Miller, Mr Stewart, younger of Stewarthall, and Mr Macintosh were my counsel, and Mr Stewart of Edinglassie my agent. I do declare that I am fully satisfied they did me justice and that no part of my misfortune was owing to their neglect or want of abilities. And as they are men of known honour, I hope they will do justice to my behaviour during the trial.

I give it as my real opinion that if Allan Breck Stewart was the murderer of Glenure that he consulted none of his friends about it.

I conclude with my solemn declaration that I tamely submit to this my lot and severe sentence, and that I freely resign my life to the will of God, who gave me my first breath, and do firmly believe that the Almighty God, who can do nothing without a good design, brought this cast of providence in my way for my spiritual good.

I die an unworthy member of the Episcopal Church of Scotland, as established before the Revolution, in full charity with all mortals, sincerely praying God may bless all my friends and relations, benefactors and well-wishers, particularly my poor wife and children, who in a special manner I recommend to His divine care and protection; and may the same God pardon and forgive all that ever did or wished me evil, as I do from my heart forgive them. I die in full hopes of mercy, not through any merit in myself, as I freely own I merit no good at the hands of my offended God; but my hope is through the blood, merits, and mediation of the ever-blessed Jesus, my Redeemer and glorious Advocate, to whom I recommend my spirit, Come, Lord Jesus, come quickly.

Mr Coupar, minister, showed me some queries a few days ago which he was desired to put to me. They are all answered already in my speech, excepting two, which are – Whether I knew Allan Breck's route from Ballachulish to Caolasnacoan, and from thence to Rannoch, before the murder happened? Answer – I declare before God I did not.

Whether I interceded with James Drummond, in the Tolbooth of Edinburgh, to persuade or entice his brother Robert, who was already outlawed, to murder Glenure, and that I would give him a good gun for that purpose, and money for carrying him off the country, and that Ardsheal's interest would procure him a commission in France? Answer – I declare before God there never passed such words betwixt James Mor Drummond and me, or any proposal to that effect.[1]

[1] *Notable Scottish Trials*, pp. 292–7.

SELECT BIBLIOGRAPHY

Arnot, Hugo, *A Collection and Abridgement of Celebrated Criminal Trials in Scotland: James Stewart in Acharn for the Murder of Colin Campbell of Glenure*, printed for the author by William Smellie, M.DCC.LXXXV

Beauchamp, Elizabeth, *The Braes of Balquhidder*, Heatherbank Press, Glasgow, 1981

Ferguson, William, *Scotland 1689 to the Present*, 'The Edinburgh History of Scotland', vol. 4, Mercat Press, 1987

Grant, I.F, *Highland Folk Ways*, Routledge & Kegan Paul Ltd., 1961; reprinted 1975

Howlett, Hamilton, *The Life and Times of Rob Roy MacGregor*, William Blackwood & Sons Ltd., Edinburgh & London, 1950

MacArthur, Lieut-General Sir William, *The Appin Murder and the Trial of James Stewart*, J.M.P. Publishing Services, London, 1960

MacGregor, A.G.M., *History of the Clan Gregor*, vol. 2, William Brown, Edinburgh, 1901

Mackay, David N. (ed.), *Notable Scottish Trials: Trial of James Stewart – The Appin Murder*, William Hodge & Co., Glasgow & Edinbugh, 1907

MacLean, Sir Fitzroy, *West Highland Tales*, William Collins & Sons Ltd., 1985; reprinted by Canongate, Edinburgh, 1990

MacLeod, Angus (ed.), *The Songs of Duncan Ban MacIntyre*, Oliver & Boyd/Scottish Gaelic Texts Society, Edinburgh, 1952

Mathieson, Angus (ed.), Transactions of the Gaelic Society of Inverness: *A Traditional Account of the Appin Murder*, vol. XXXV,

1929–30, Gaelic Society/Northern Counties Printing & Publishing Co. Ltd., Inverness, 1939

Murray, W.H., *Rob Roy MacGregor – His Life and Times*, Richard Drew Publishing, Glasgow, 1982

Starforth, Michael (advised by Stuart and Yvonne Carmichael), *Clan Stewart of Appin, 1463–1752, and its Unfailing Loyalty to the Royal House of Stewart*, Appin Historical Society c/o Dunvegan, Argyll, 1997

INDEX

Aberdeen, 29, 64, 136

Aberfoyle, 78

Achindarroch, 59, 67

Aldavoin, 108

Allward, Lt. Colonel Stewart, 19

Annat, 71

Appin, 13-4, 16, 17, 19, 20, 30, 31, 33, 34,
    44, 47, 50, 51, 64, 69, 70, 73, 77, 82, 85,
    86, 87, 88, 89, 90, 91, 99, 106, 118, 122,
    123, 131, 138, 141, 142, 147

Appin House (Lettershuna), 134

Appin Regiment, 41, 49, 50, 56, 64, 134

Archarn (farm of), 58, 59, 67, 68, 73, 81, 82,
    84, 88, 96, 104–6, 107, 113, 116, 124,
    126, 129, 133, 139

Ardchattan, 14, 99, 131, 144
    Church, 131

Ardchattan Priory, 98–9

Ardnamurchan, 32

Ardsheal estate, 30, 56, 59, 64, 67, 69, 71,
    72, 75-6, 79, 84, 85, 87, 103, 125, 139,
    147, 148

Ardsheal House, 51, 52, 54

Argyll, 14, 19, 32, 36, 65, 71, 81

Argyll,
    Agnes, Countess of,
    Archibald Campbell, 2nd Earl of, 19
    Archibald Campbell, 7th Earl of, 24–9
    Archibald Campbell, 8th Earl & Marquis
        of, 32
    Archibald Campbell (Lord Islay), 3rd
        Duke of, 37, 116, 117, 118, 119,
        126–8
    Colin Campbell, 1st Earl of, 15, 16
    Colin Campbell., 6th Earl of, 24
    John Campbell, 2nd Duke of, 36, 37

John Campbell of Mamore, Major-
    General, 4th Duke of, 45, 46, 47, 48, 49,
    52, 77–8

John Campbell of Mamore ('Colonel
    Jack'), 5th Duke of, 45, 46

Argyllshire Militia, 44–8

Argyllshire, sheriff-depute of,

Army of the Covenant, 34

Arran, Earl of, 20

Atholl Raid (the), 48

Auchterarder, 37

Auldearn, battle of, 33

Baird, Sergeant, 115

Balfron, 78

Ballachulish, 19, 20, 102, 142, 152
    Bridge, 129, 131
    Ferry, 13, 20, 83, 86, 127
    House, 83, 84, 88–9, 92, 135, 142

Ballieveolan (now Drimavuich), 66

Balquhidder, 38, 39, 42

Bannockburn, battle of, 43

Barcaldine, 17, 63
    Castle, 30, 33, 115, 134

Baron Kennedy of Dunure, 76

Barons Court, 63, 76

Barons of Exchequer (the), 63, 64, 66, 139,
    140, 146

Beinn a Bheithir, 53, 133

Benderloch, 17, 30

birlinn, 31

Black Book of Taymouth, The, 30

Black Friday, 43

Black Watch, the, 78

Blair Atholl, 32, 64

Blair Castle, 42

Boinne na Gibbet (Rock of the Gibbet), 131

'Bonnie Dundee', *see* Graham, James
Bothwell, Francis Stewart (Earl of), 27
Breadalbane, John Campbell (1st Earl
   of), 36, 44
Brown, George of Coalston (sheriff
   of Forfar), 118, 126, 151
Buchanan (messenger), 53
Bury, Lord, 111–2
Callander, 42
Callart, 64, 85
Cameron of Callart, 83, 84, 109
Cameron of Fassifern, 66
Cameron of Glen Nevis, 104, 105
Cameron of Lochiel, Donald, 36, 44, 46,
   63, 66, 81–2, 85
Cameron of Lochiel, Sir Ewan, 63
Campbell of Achallader, John, 132
Campbell of Achnaba, Patrick (surgeon), 98
Campbell of Airds, 67, 82, 113
Campbell of Airds, John (3rd of), 34
Campbell of Ardchattan, Alexander, 144
Campbell of Ardkinlass, Sir James, 24–5
Campbell of Ardnamurchan, *see* Campbell
   of Barbreck
Campbell of Asnich, Robert, 117
Campbell of Auchinbreck, Sir Duncan, 33
Campbell of Auchinbreck, Sir Dougal, 24
Campbell of Auchinsicallan, Patrick, 114
Campbell of Ballieveolan, 66, 67, 68, 71,
   92, 97
Campbell of Barbreck, Sir Donald, 31–2
Campbell of Barcaldine, Duncan
   (sheriff), 115
Campbell of Barcaldine, John, 63, 64,
   81, 114, 123, 132, 137, 139, 141
Campbell of Cabrachan, John Oig, 27–8
Campbell of Calder (Cawdor), Sir John,
   24–8, 31
Campbell of Dunstaffnage (Captain), 33
Campbell of Ederline, Neil (Bishop of
   Argyll), 24
Campbell of Glenorchy, Sir Duncan
   (2nd of), 19
Campbell of Glenorchy, Sir Duncan (7th
   of), 24–6, 30
Campbell of Glenorchy, Sir Robert, 31
Campbell of Glenure, Colin, 13, 46, 48–9,
   63–9, 75–6, 78, 79, 80–2, 83, 85–95,
96–9, 102, 103, 108, 112–3, 115, 116,
   117, 118–9, 122, 125, 126, 128, 130,
   132, 133, 135, 136, 137, 138, 139, 140,
   144, 146–7, 149, 150–2
Campbell of Knockbuy, 48–9
Campbell of Levenside, John,
Campbell of Lochnell, Archibald, 24–9, 31
Campbell of Lundy, Colin (brother of 7th
   Earl of Argyll), 26
Campbell of Octomore, Donald, 47
Campbell of Southhall (juryman), 126, 150
Campbell of Stonefield, Archibald (sheriff-
   depute of Argyll), 122
Campbell, Alexander (brother of Glenure),
   136
Campbell, Alexander (inn-keeper), 74–5, 150
Campbell, Alexander (minister of Inveraray),
   150–1
Campbell, Alexander (surgeon), 98
Campbell, 'Colonel Jack', *see* 5th Duke of
   Argyll
Campbell, Duncan (inn-keeper), 71–2
Campbell, Duncan (sheriff), 115
Campbell, Elizabeth (daughter of Glenure),
   65, 117
Campbell, James (clerk), 126
Campbell, Janet (wife of Glenure), 65, 98,
   117, 118, 119
Campbell, John of Mamore, Major-General,
   see 4th Duke of Argyll
Campbell, John (younger of Levenside), 117
Campbell, Lucy (daughter of Glenure), 65,
   117
Campbell, Margaret (widow of John Oig),
   28
Campbell, Mungo (nephew of Glenure), 81,
   83, 93–5, 115, 122, 137
Caolas Mhic Pharuig (ferry Lochaber shore),
   90–1
Caolasnacoan ('Narrows of the Dog'), 103,
   106, 124, 146, 147, 152
Carmichaels, 21
Carnoch, 83
Castle Stalker, 18–9, 33, 34, 35, 47, 48
Chapeau, Capt. David, 114–5
Charles I, 32, 34
Charles II, 34
Churchill, General, 72, 112

Index

Cnap a'Cholais, 129

Committee of Estates, 34

Connel Ferry, 17, 30

Cope, General John, 42

Cormorant's Rock, 18

Corran Ferry, 48

Corrieyairack Pass, 42

Corrynakeigh (heugh of), 107, 108

Coupar, the Rev., 152

Crawford, Colonel John, 71, 111, 112, 115, 133, 148–9

Crieff, 46

Cuil Bay, 56

Culloden, battle of, 49, 51, 60, 64, 70, 78, 112, 134, 135

Cumberland, William (Duke of), 46, 47

Dalnacardoch Forest, 42

Derby, 43

Dewar Manuscripts, 41, 91

Donibristle Castle, 27

Douglas, William, *see* Morton, Earl of

Doune, 40

Drummond, James Mor, *see* MacGregor, James Mor

Duart Castle, 4, 19, 21

Dumbarton, 45, 46

Dunblane, 46

Dunkeld, 35

Dunollie Castle, 28

Dunstaffnage Castle, 16, 18, 33, 48

Duror, 20, 21, 118

Earl Marischal of Scotland, George Keith, 55

Eas nan Con (cave), 53

Edinburgh, 34, 41, 42, 60, 72, 74, 75, 76, 77, 79, 80, 81, 103, 111, 116, 141, 146

Tolbooth, 77, 78, 139, 152

Elchies, Lord, 117

Erskine, James (sheriff-depute), 117, 120

Falkirk, battle of, 44, 45

farming, 56–9, 88

Fasnacloich, 82, 133

House, 104

Ferguson, Sir James (Lord Kilkerran), 117

Fife, 27

Flanders, 54

Fletcher of Crannach, 45–5

Flodden, battle of, 20

Fontenoy, battle of, 46, 78

Forbes, Bishop, 129–30

Fort George, 47

Fort William, 47, 48, 49, 53, 74, 77, 81, 83, 104, 106, 109, 111, 113, 114, 115, 116, 120, 127, 129, 133, 134, 148 *see also* Maryburgh

Fraser, Simon (Master of Lovat), 117–8, 119

George I, 36, 42

George II, 44, 49, 61, 64, 65, 66

Glasgow, 43

Gleann a Chaolais, 89

Gleann an Fhiodh (Glen of the Wood), 81, 91, 98

Gleann Salach, 99, 135

Glen Creran, 14, 51, 54, 65, 81, 82, 99, 133

Glen Duror, 42, 54, 55, 56, 59, 66, 67, 87, 134; store of, 59, 79, 97

Glen Etive, 54

Glen Ogle, 75

Glen Shira, 36

Glencoe, 14, 18, 74, 83, 103, 106, 108, 137, 144

Glenfinnan, 42

Glenlivet, 29

Glenorchy, 18, 45

Glenorchy, John Lord (2nd Earl of Breadalbane), 44, 45

Glenorchy, John Lord (3rd Earl of Breadalbane), 63, 64

Glenstockdale, 51, 52

Glenstrae, 25

Glenure, 65, 80, 81

House, 65, 80, 81, 98

Gordon of Auchintoul, General Alexander, 36

Gordon, George, *see* Huntly, 4th Earl of

Graham of Drunkie, 78

Graham, James of Claverhouse ('Bonnie Dundee'), 35

Grant of Prestongrange, William (Lord Advocate), 117, 120, 125, 126

Gregorian Calendar, 116

Guthrie, James (Dingwall Pursuivant), 34

Haining, Lord, 80

Hawley, Lt. General Henry, 44, 46

Holyrood House, 27

Howard, Colonel, 111

Huntly, George Gordon (4th Earl of), 24,

26–7, 29

Inshaig, 105

Inveraray, 32, 36, 37, 46, 48, 81, 86, 108,
    111, 116, 120, 123, 126, 147, 148
    Castle, 37, 42

Inverlochy, 19, 33

Inverness, 47, 48

Islay, 47

Islay, Lord, *see* Argyll, Archibald Campbell,
    3rd Duke of

Jacobite Rising
    (1715), 36, 41, 55, 104, 128, 149
    (1719), 55, 128, 149
    (1745), 41–50, 56, 61, 63, 73, 99, 118,
        128, 134, 149

James III, 17

James IV, 18, 20

James V, 20

James VI & I, 26, 29

James VII & II, 34

James VIII & III, 36, 37, 41, 55

Keil Chapel, 131, 143

Keith, George (Earl Marischal of Scotland),
    55

Kennedy, Baron (of Dunure), 76–7

Kennedy, Donald (sheriff's officer), 81, 86,
    91, 92, 94–5, 97, 135

Kentallen, 71, 86, 88, 91
    Inn, 92, 95, 96

Keppoch, 18

Key, Jean, *see* Wright, Jean

Kilcumun, 33

Killiecrankie, battle of, 35

Kilsyth, battle of, 33

Kintalline, 67

Kirkton, 39

Knepoch (Knipoch), 27

Lagan Bhlàr an Lochain, 135

Lagnaha, 53, 148

Lanrick, 42

Larach, 97, 106

Leith, 54, 60, 141

Leslie, Lt. Gen. David (Lord Newark), 34

Lettermore, 51, 93
    farm of, 67
    wood of, 84, 87, 91, 95, 108, 119, 133

Lettershuna, *see* Appin House

Lismore, 48

Livingstone, John Roy, 88

Loch Awe, 15, 25, 48
    Lordship of, 26

Loch Creran, 17, 30, 66, 99

Loch Doine, 38

Loch Etive, 17, 80, 89, 98–9, 131, 137

Loch Feochan, 27

Loch Fyne, 37

Loch Leven, 21, 26, 54, 81, 84, 86, 90, 106

Loch Linnhe, 14, 48, 51, 56, 131, 143

Loch Rannoch, 46

Lochaber, 19, 82, 83, 84, 89, 90, 138
    Braes of, 86

Lochearnhead, 75

London, 43

Lorn, 14, 30
    Lordship of, 15–7

Loudoun Castle, 55

Loudoun, John Campbell (4th Earl of), 42,
    46, 49

Lovat, Lord, 118

MacArthur, General, 135

MacColl, Dugald, 67–9, 72–3, 104, 105,
    114–5, 123, 133, 147

MacColl, Dugald (of the Locks), 135

MacColl, John Beg, 69, 85–8, 104, 105,
    113, 114–5, 120, 123, 147

MacColl, John Breck (bouman), 106–7,
    108–10, 115, 122, 124, 137, 147

MacColl, John (inn-keeper's servant), 72

MacColl, John Mor, 69, 72–3, 82, 86, 123,
    147

MacColl, Katherine (servant), 105

MacColl, Katherine (of Coalisnacoan), 107

MacColl, Malcolm (inn-keeper), 72

MacColl, Red Ewan (Ewan Roy), 122–3,
    137, 147

MacColl, Sorley, 19

Maccombich, Duncan, 148

Maccombich, John (miller), 148

Maccombie, John Breck, 67, 86, 88

Maccombie, John, 68

MacCoull, Alan, 16

MacDonald of Moidart, 30

MacDonald, Alasdair MacColla, 32

MacDonald, John (of Glencoe), 83, 103, 137

MacDonald, Isabel, 83, 103, 115

MacDonalds

of Clanranald, 36
of Glengarry, 36
MacDougall, Duncan (of Dunollie), 26, 28
Macfarlane, John, W.S., 112, 119
MacGregor
  of Glencarnock, 42
  of Glengyle, 36
MacGregor, James Mor, 36, 37, 39–40, 43,
  77–9, 133, 139–42, 152
MacGregor, Malcolm (of Marchfield), 38
MacGregor, Rob Roy, 36, 37, 38, 39, 42,
  77, 139, 140
MacGregor, Robin Oig, 39–40, 77, 78–9,
  132, 139–40, 141, 142, 152
MacGregor, Ronald, 40
Macinnes, Archibald (the *portair cam*), 89
Macinnes, Katherine, 102
MacIntyre, Donald, 138–9
MacIntyre, Duncan Ban (poet of
  Glenorchy), 44–5, 58, 99–101
MacIntyre, Mor, 88
Mackay of Bighouse (the Hon. Hugh), 65
Mackellar, Mary, 134
MacKenzie, 'Grey Ewan', 88
MacKenzie, John (servant of Glenure), 81,
  86, 89–90, 91–2, 94–7
Mackintosh, Robert (advocate), 118, 119,
  151
MacLaren of Ardveich, 15, 38, 138
MacLaren, Colin (merchant), 74–6, 150–1
MacLaren, John (Baron Stob Chon), 38–40,
  77, 78, 139
MacLean of Duart, Lachlan, 19, 26, 36
Macleay of Bachuill, 19
Macleod of Macleod,
MacPhee (the mad), 131
Maitland, John, *see* Thirlestane, Lord
Mamore, 19, 64, 77, 85
Mar, John Erskine (6th Earl of), 36
Marchfield estate, 38
Mary Queen of Scots, 25, 26, 27
Maryburgh, 47, 77, 81, 85, 86, 88, 89, 105,
  109, 123, *see also* Fort William
Miller, Thomas (advocate), 118, 121, 151
Moidart, 41
Montrose, Marquis of, 32
Moor of Rannoch, 18, 46, 136
Moray, Countess of, 25

Moray, James Stewart (2nd Earl of), 24–9
Morton, William Douglas (Earl of), 26, 28
muileartach (miller of Leith), 59, 79
Murray, Ewan (inn-keeper), 75–6, 151
Murray, Lord George, 42, 45–6, 49
Oban, 27, 28, 38
Onich, 86
Pelham, Chancellor of the Exchequer, 140
Penrith, 43
Perth, 37, 42, 44, 46
  Duke of, 42, 77
Philiphaugh, battle of, 33
Pinkie, battle of, 20
Port Seton, 42
Portnacroish, 72
  church, 17
  inn, 72
Portsonachan, 48
Prestonpans, battle of, 70
Pultney, General, 114
Ranken, Donald, 124, 148
Rannoch, 70, 81, 152
Reay, Lord, 65
Rosneath, 28
St Mary's Episcopal Church, 142
St Moluag, church of Lismore, 19
Scott, Captain Caroline Frederick, 47–8, 52,
  53
Scott, Sir Walter, 141
Sheriffmuir, battle of, 37
South Shian Ferry, 30
Stalk, battle of, 17
Stalker, castle, *see* Castle Stalker
Stewart of Ardnamurchan, 67–8
Stewart of Ardvorlich, 34
Stewart of Edinglassie (lawyer), 116, 151
Stewart of Glenbuckie, 67
Stewart of Invernahyle, 38
Stewart, Alexander (4th of Invernahyle), 33,
  39
Stewart, Alexander (of Ballachulish), 35
Stewart, Alexander ('old Ballachulish'), 87,
  91–2, 97, 102, 115, 135
Stewart, Alexander (packman), 104, 105–6,
  107–8, 109–10, 123, 147–8
Stewart, Allan (3rd of Appin), 19–24
Stewart, Allan (son of James of the Glen),
  66–7, 70, 82, 105, 106, 108, 110, 111,

113, 124, 132–3

Stewart, Allan Breck, 42, 43, 50, 59, 60, 70–3, 79, 81–4, 88–9, 91, 102–10, 112–6, 118, 119, 121, 122, 124, 125, 126, 132–3, 140–2, 144, 146, 147, 152

Stewart, Anne (daughter of Charles, 5th of Ardsheal), 52, 60

Stewart, Charles (5th of Ardsheal), 41–4, 46, 50–4, 55, 56, 59–61, 64, 66, 67, 69, 83, 103, 112, 124, 134, 140, 146, 149–50, 152

Stewart, Charles (7th of Ballachulish), 142

Stewart, Charles (lawyer), 77, 85, 86, 104, 113, 123, 148,

Stewart, Charles (son of James of the Glen), 70, 83, 112, 133

Stewart, Donald (nephew of 'old Ballachulish'), 97, 102–3, 134–6, 146

Stewart, Donald 'of the Hammers' (2nd of Invernahyle), 20

Stewart, Dugald (1st of Appin), 16, 18

Stewart, Dugald (10th of Appin), 41, 56, 61, 64, 83, 106, 113, 134

Stewart, Duncan (2nd of Appin), 18, 19

Stewart, Duncan (2nd of Ardsheal), 33, 50

Stewart, Duncan (4th of Appin), 20

Stewart, Duncan (son of Robert the miller), 96

Stewart, Duncan 'Baothaire' (7th of Appin), 31

Stewart, Duncan Mor (8th of Appin), 33

Stewart, Elizabeth (daughter of James of the Glen), 70, 104, 133

Stewart, Francis, see Bothwell, Earl of

Stewart, Henry (suicide's grave), 142

Stewart, Hugh, 79

Stewart, Hugh (lodging-house keeper), 141

Stewart, Isabel (wife of Charles, 5th of Ardsheal), 15, 42, 51–4, 60

Stewart, James, see Moray, 2nd Earl of

Stewart, James (1st of Fasnacloich), 20

Stewart, James ('old Fasnacloich'), 35, 133, 136–9

Stewart, James (younger of Fasnacloich), 47, 49, 81, 82, 83, 115, 136–7

Stewart, James (Regent), 25

Stewart, James of the Glen (Seumas a' Ghlinne), 13, 36, 37, 42, 43, 50, 51,

55–7, 59, 60–1, 64–5, 66–72, 74, 78–9, 80, 82, 83, 85, 88, 96–7, 102, 103–4, 105–6, 108, 110, 111–32, 132, 134, 139, 140, 141, 143

Stewart, John (of Achnacon), 71, 72

Stewart, John (1st of Ardsheal, tutor of Robert 9th of Appin), 30, 34, 35, 36, 39

Stewart, John (4th of Ardsheal), 55

Stewart, John (Lord of Lorn), 15, 38, 138

Stewart, John ('young Ballachulish'), 67, 68, 84, 104, 115, 131, 132, 134, 148

Stewart, John 'Gordonich Ban' (5th of Appin), 24, 26, 29, 30, 31

Stewart, Lilias (daugher of young Ballachulish), 131, 143

Stewart, Margaret (sister of the packman), 106

Stewart, Margaret (wife of James of the Glen), 59, 67, 68, 83, 97, 104–6, 107–8, 114, 131

Stewart, Mary (daughter of Fasnacloich), 133

Stewart, Prince Charles Edward, 41, 42, 43, 44, 45–6, 47, 49, 60, 70, 73, 112, 134

Stewart, Robert (9th of Appin), 34, 35, 36, 38, 41

Stewart, Robert (miller), 96

Stewart, Walter (briefly Lord of Lorn), 16–7

Stewart, Walter (younger of Stewarthall), 118, 119, 151

Stewart, William (Maryburgh merchant), 59, 86, 88, 103–4, 105, 109, 123, 125, 126, 147, 148

Stewarts of Innermeath, see Lordship of Lorn

Stirling, 29, 36, 37, 44, 74, 75

  Castle, 44, 45–6

Stob Chon (Hound's Peak), 38

Tay Bridge, 48

Taycreggan, 48

Tayinluib inn, 74

Thirlestane, John Maitland (Lord), 26, 28

Tigh-phuirt, 137

Treaty of Union, 55

Tullibardine, Lord, 55

Victory, the, 48

West Highland Tales, 138

Wester Invernenty, farm of, 38–9

William III, 35

Wright, Jean, 78, 142